D0627385

The Open University Opens

Books by Jeremy Tunstall

The Fishermen
The Advertising Man
Old and Alone
The Westminster Lobby Correspondents
Journalists at Work

The Open University Opens

edited by
Jeremy Tunstall

University of Massachusetts Press
Amherst

First published in 1974
by Routledge & Kegan Paul Ltd
Broadway House, 68-74 Carter Lane,
London EC4V 5EL
(c) Jeremy Tunstall 1974
Printed in the United States of America
Library of Congress Catalog Card Number 74-78983
ISBN (cloth) 0-87023-167-7
ISBN (paper) 0-87023-168-5

Contents

Introduction   *Jeremy Tunstall*   **vii**

Part I   Interim history

1   *An interim history of the Open University*
     Brian MacArthur   3

Part II   Implications

2   *The economic implications   Leslie Wagner*   21
3   *The seeds of radical change   Willem van der Eyken*   28
4   *A view from New England   Norman Birnbaum*   34

Part III   The students and the system

5   *Admissions policy   Ray Thomas*   47
6   *The OU student   Naomi McIntosh*   54
7   *The OU in the south-west   Dudley Buckingham*   66
8   *Evaluation for the OU   David Hawkridge*   70
9   *Accounting for themselves   Jennifer Rogers*   77

Part IV   Some students

10   *Welsh hill farmer   J. Elwyn Hughes*   85
11   *Secretary   Valerie Saunders*   87
12   *My hobby   Michael Gardner*   90
13   *Married couple   Stan and Dinah Penman*   92
14   *Housewife with five children   Jill MacKean*   95

15 *Local councillor   Elizabeth Murphy*   97
16 *Music teacher   Millicent Sherwood*   99
17 *Older student   Arthur McTaggart-Short*   102
18 *Perpetual student   J. Philpott*   104
19 *Factory worker   Tom Wellman*   106
20 *Insurance manager   Jack Mainwaring*   108
21 *Remote student   Barbara Abraham*   110

Part V Teachers and courses

22 *Divide and teach: The new division of labour*
    Francis Castles   115
23 *The OU academic: Graeme Salaman and*
    Kenneth Thompson   120
24 *Course production at the OU: Basic problems and*
    activities   Brian N. Lewis   125
25 *The making of D100: A view from the social science*
    Faculty   Michael Drake   135
26 *A view from the science Faculty   Peter J. Smith*   140
27 *A view from the mathematics Faculty   G. A. Read*   145
28 *A view from the technology Faculty*
    G. S. Holister   149
29 *A view from the educational studies Faculty*
    Phillip Williams   153
30 *A view from the arts Faculty   Arthur Marwick*   158

Part VI The media

31 *The OU publishing operation   Hamish MacGibbon* 165
32 *Broadcasting and multi-media teaching*
    Anthony Bates   170
33 *New media in the OU: An international perspective*
    Richard Hooper   178

    A selected bibliography   185
    Index   187

Introduction

The Open University breaks away from so many traditions of British higher education that one should, perhaps, not be startled by the extreme nature of the attitudes expressed both for and against it. The use of BBC radio and television in the teaching may play some part in shaping extreme attitudes—these media often attract passionate responses, in educational, as much as in entertainment, programming.

The Open University is so drastically different from other British universities and in so many ways that it seems essential to list some of its basic characteristics: *The Open University is basically a correspondence university*. The students are 'independent learners' working largely in their own homes. They receive teaching materials, and return their work, by post.

The Open University uses broadcasting and other media. It puts on radio and television programmes which are integrated with written materials and transmitted by the BBC at off-peak times; these broadcasts are intended to take up roughly 5 to 8 per cent of student study time. The OU runs a substantial book publishing operation: 'correspondence' materials are published in book form. There are also unusual teaching materials, such as 'home experimental kits' which science students receive and which include, for instance, a microscope.

OU students are adults mostly in their twenties, thirties, or forties (A small pilot scheme for eighteen-year-olds begins in 1974.) The large majority are in full-time employment. All OU students are part time.

There are no entrance qualifications. Unlike other British universities, the OU does not demand two or three 'A' levels from applicants. Particularly in the first year, the majority of students either had this level of qualification or something higher—for instance a schoolteaching non-degree qualification. About one-third of students have indeed been admitted without the formal qualifications which other British universities require.

The OU is a nationally spread organization. Students are fairly evenly spread in all parts of Britain, from Cornwall and Devon to Scotland.

The OU has an unusual timetable. The OU operates on a calendar year beginning in January, with final examinations in November. There are no terms or semesters; there are no lectures and no conventional timetable clashes. Students can also proceed at their own pace—normally taking between two and eight years to earn a degree.

The OU operates a credit system—unlike any other British university. Six credits are required for a pass degree and eight credits for an honours degree. A one-credit course requires roughly ten hours of student time per week, or a total of about 350 hours. 'Credit exemptions' are granted for students who have specific professional or other qualifications.

The teaching arrangements involve a new division of labour. Central academic staff work, not individually, but as part of a 'course team'; they prepare 'correspondence units' which are printed, and broadcast programmes, which are recorded, and each course is then 'replayed' for a total of four years. Regionally a large counselling and teaching force is employed on a part-time basis. Students can meet counsellors at local 'study centres'— rooms usually rented from local colleges; for each course students have 'course tutors' who mark their essays or other written work and who are normally available for some evening or weekend tutorial classes. One-week summer schools, compulsory for some courses, are also staffed mainly by part-time teachers.

The OU is computer based. The OU presents administrative problems of a scale and complexity seldom previously encountered in British higher education. Inevitably a computer plays a central part not only in processing *Computer-marked assignments* (CMAS) but also, for example, in operating the mailing schedule.

Economies of scale. The OU is large; in 1973 it had about 35,000 part-time students, about 1,600 full-time employees and several thousand part-time teaching and counselling staff. It is also cheap because it does without lecture theatres, residential facilities and some other expensive aspects of conventional British universities.

Although the failure rate is substantial, it is relatively low for part-time higher education. Consequently, the ou is a way of producing graduates much more cheaply than do conventional British universities.

The O U has no student campus. Students never come together on a permanent campus or campuses. The headquarters of the ou, where the academics are heavily outnumbered by administrative and service personnel, is near Bletchley and within the new town of Milton Keynes, 45 miles north west of London.

Economies: of scale, and other. Leslie Wagner indicates (p. 21) the major reasons for the cost-effectiveness of the Open University as compared with other British universities. British universities are predominantly residential, and providing residential accommodation for students for only thirty weeks out of the fifty-two each year is an expensive business. In ordinary British universities the teaching arrangements are extremely lavish. Moreover, many of the elaborate lecture theatres and laboratories in both British universities and polytechnics, even in the weeks when they are in use, are used for relatively few hours each week. The Open University produces major economies because ou students live at home; the ou abolishes not only lecture theatres but also lecturers in the conventional sense. Course materials are produced centrally by a relatively small academic staff. While in 1973 one British academic in an ordinary university taught about eight full-time students, one ou central academic taught about 180 part-time students. (In addition, the ou uses an army of part-time teachers.) Thus in addition to the *capital cost* savings, there are also very large savings on *current costs*.

The ou in its third year of teaching was already the largest British university in the sense that by 1973 it had more part-time students than London University had full-time students. But compared with most other industrialized countries, and especially the usa, the British ou is not particularly large. In the modest movement which has occurred in Britain towards mass higher education, the general policy has been to extend Oxford and Cambridge standards to all universities—especially in the provision of 'hotel facilities' and the ratio of one full-time academic to eight students (although polytechnic students are less luxuriously treated). In Britain the annual cost to the state of a university student roughly equals the annual earnings of an industrial worker.

The Open University itself engages in some fairly expensive activities. One is the provision of face-to-face teaching on a limited, optional, basis. Another example is the high quality of OU printed course units and other materials (see MacGibbon, p. 165). Compared with commercial publishing, the OU publishing operation is certainly an expensive one—especially in terms of artwork and colour printing. But even should the hoped-for substantial outside sales not result, this publishing operation is cheap when compared with the lecture system for which it substitutes. (A question for conventional universities: Is it desirable that such tiny proportions of the total cost of graduates should go into paying for books which the student acquires as his own?)

Broadcasting is another fairly expensive component within an overall low-cost strategy. OU broadcasting in 1973 cost nearly £2 million. But that is only about £50 per student per year. Broadcasting is one of the reasons why the Open University has not yet reaped all of the potential economies of scale. Student numbers could be doubled from 35,000 to 70,000, with only about a 50 per cent increase in total costs. Additional economies of scale are substantial at 55,000 and there are further economies with 70,000 students. But 35,000 or 70,000 is not necessarily the optimum total number of students. Even if some diminishing return elements emerged (and it is difficult to see what these would be) most of the economies of scale could still be reaped with several times 70,000 students. The 'conventional' State University of New York in 1971–2 had no less than 120,000 part-time students, in addition to 226,000 full-time students.

Is it really Open?

Lord Crowther in his 1969 inaugural address as Chancellor of the Open University stated that it was open 'as to people'; 'as to places'; 'as to methods'; and finally 'to ideas'. Debate has subsequently centred on the first of these: Is the openness of the OU more than a facade?

One can list other ways in which the Open University is open. It can claim to be open in the sense of being flexible for the differing requirements of different students; it is possible to go fast or slow, to stop and start, to take unusual combinations of courses, to re-take failed courses, or to 'drop in' again after having 'dropped out'.| The ou is also open in a goldfish-bowl sense. People can look in from the outside and see how the fish swim. The broadcasts go out over public national networks. The basic course materials (the 'units' and 'blocks' of 'correspondence' material) are available on general sale and indeed vigorously marketed. Part-time teachers from nearly all British universities and polytechnics—and many of the colleges of education and further education—take part in the teaching and examining. 'Outside' academics also work as consultants in various ways. Nevertheless, I would argue that, apart from the part-time teachers, few outsiders get more than a glimpse of one part of the overall system (for example, seeing only one or two units, or one or two programmes).

'Open as to people'? The most consistent line of criticism has been that the ou has failed to provide a 'second chance' to large numbers of working-class adults; by insisting on being a *university*, it is said, the Open University has inevitably catered for middle-class teachers, housewives and the like. Martin Trow and others reply that this is an argument for an Open Technical College as well, but not a fair argument against an Open University. Naomi McIntosh's article contains evidence (pp. 60–3) relevant to this argument, in particular. Most 1971 and 1972 entrants were in middle-class occupations; however, the majority of these students had working-class fathers and could thus claim to be of working-class origin; the high proportion of 1971 entrants who were schoolteachers and in other middle-class occupations declined in 1972.

Tyrrell Burgess argues that the Open University is typical of other universities in that its basic objectives are extremely vague. This is a rather simple-minded comment—as even a passing acquaintance with the existing body of knowledge about organizations would reveal. The report of the Planning Committee, like Brian MacArthur's (p. 3) account of the political history of the project, makes clear that the Open University was the result of a coalition of widely different interests and people. The report of the Planning Committee was one more in a long line of official educational reports during the 1960s (Crowther, Robbins, Newsom, Plowden, Dainton, Swann); it was firmly within this British tradition in being liberal expansionist in tone, empirical and specific as to numbers and money, vague as to overall goal.

In general the forecasts of the Planning Committee—such as a heavy demand from schoolteachers—have been fulfilled. Neither Harold Wilson nor Jennie Lee, who gave political birth to the OU, ever expected large proportions of manual workers to come flocking off the factory floor. But this is not to deny that 'open as to people' poses real dilemmas and choices for the Open University. Ray Thomas (p. 47), a specialist on the economics of new towns, shows that, like other aspects of social policy, the selection process may favour middle-class applicants to a greater extent than is at first obvious.

Is it really a University?

The OU clearly has all the minimum characteristics of a university. It has students and professors, it sets examinations and awards degrees, it has several faculties and one Royal Charter. On the other hand it also clearly lacks many things found in all other British universities.

How good are its teaching staff? One common way of comparing the academic staff of universities is by looking at their higher degrees. In Britain this varies greatly between science on the one hand and social sciences and arts on the other; in the latter fields doctorates are a relative innovation. Nevertheless, here below are comparative figures for doctorates of all British university teachers in 1969–70 from an article by John Bilby (in *Higher Education Review*, 1971):

	(%)
Oxford and Cambridge	65
'New' universities	55
London University	54
Old Civic	53
Wales	51
Young Civic	51
Scotland	48
Former CAT	42
All universities	52

All categories of universities are fairly close to the average of 52 per cent with doctorates. Where does the Open University come in this? A count of all 164 ou academic staff in post in late 1972 (counting part-timers as half) showed 98·5 to have doctorates—that is 60 per cent. In so far as it shows anything, it suggests that ou central academics are well within the general range for British university teachers, and probably in the top half of the table. A second criterion which is often adopted is number of books and articles published. Since considerable emphasis was placed on writing ability and output when ou academics were being re-cruited, on this criterion, also, one might expect them to show up well on a league table.

What about the quality of Open University degrees? The ou is following the pattern standard to all British universities of appointing eminent academics from other universities to its examining boards; those academics have a decisive voice and ensure that the standards of all British degrees are roughly similar. Viewed from a United States perspective all British universities are in effect campuses of a single national university—and such variations in quality as undoubtedly exist are comparable to, say, variations in quality between campuses of the single University of California.

But ou degrees will certainly differ in detail from some other degrees, especially single discipline degrees elsewhere. Despite the interdisciplinary emphasis and the effective range of choice, however, many degrees will in practice be similar to 'joint' (or two discipline degrees) elsewhere. Many ou students will settle for six credit 'pass' degrees and these will be comparable to pass degrees in Scotland and elsewhere. It is, of course, the eight credit 'honours' degrees which will be comparable to the normal British honours degree.

Does the Open University offer a range of facilities to students which one would normally expect of a British university? Obviously not. It does not provide its own hotel facilities, teaching buildings, and libraries. Nor does it provide its students with theatres, tennis courts, football fields, subsidized drinking facilities and the like. But these extra-curricular facilities which students lack, are also not found in many universities in other countries. Nor does the consequent lack of theatrical or sporting activity reflect a lack of interest in these things on the part of Open University students; there are indeed professional actors and sportsmen within the study body. Busy adult students would presumably not be reluctant to accept such activities—if both the leisure facilities and also the paid leisure time itself were provided by the taxpayers.

What many o u students would probably say they do miss most, however, is more personal contact with teachers and other students in reasonably pleasant surroundings. While not minimizing these very important and deeply felt lacks in the Open University system, there are a few ways in which o u students receive (something *superior* in comparison even with full-time residential British students:

1 They receive more carefully prepared teaching materials.

2 The average o u course includes in its broadcasts a number of leading academics from British and other universities. Often these people are the authors of set texts for the course. A number of Open University courses must already have employed a greater range of academic talents than has ever been collected together in preparing a single course in that particular discipline anywhere in the world.*

3 Open University students do not have access to a university library. But all university teachers know that relatively few students make much use of scarce copies of journals; and all students know that university libraries hold few copies of basic texts.) The Open University has accepted this standard situation much more realistically and effectively than is usual in British universities; consequently many o u students get a superior bargain. 'Readers' are specially edited and published for o u students; cheap editions of prescribed texts are specially negotiated with publishers; and students are sent their personal offprint copies of key journal articles and similar materials.

Obviously the o u shares some characteristics with polytechnics —and it will share more if it comes to concentrate heavily on 'post-experience' non-degree courses. The o u's future will be dependent not only upon the future shape of universities and polytechnics but also the future shape of teacher training and adult, and further, education in general. The influence is also

---

* An example from my own experience in 'The Sociological Perspective', a half-course. Distinguished outsiders who contributed in broadcasts included: Raymond Aron, Howard Becker, Tom Bottomore, Aaron Cicourel, Percy Cohen, Ronald Fletcher, Alvin Gouldner, David Martin, Robert Nisbet and Raymond Williams.

likely to operate in the other direction as Willem van der Eyken (p. 28) points out.

What exactly is the difference between a British polytechnic and a university? Polytechnics differ from both the o u and other British universities in lacking the automony to devise and award their own degrees. But like the Open University the polytechnics are producing graduates, and they are doing so more cheaply than the conventional universities; moreover the c n a a (Council for National Academic Awards) arrangements are likely to ensure that polytechnic graduates are of a comparable standard to graduates of conventional universities. Thus the polytechnics, like the Open University, pose awkward questions for the conventional universities. The polytechnics are also criticized for copying the conventional universities too closely and for not having more working-class students.

The polytechnics, in turn, pose awkward questions for the Open University (and vice versa). For example: What are the implications of the polytechnics moving towards a greater emphasis on degree courses, while at the same time the o u intends to place some emphasis on 'post-experience' non-degree courses? What happens if the polytechnics, using conventional laboratories, are able to produce science and technology graduates as cheaply as the Open University?

The o u will probably continue for some years to be in an often awkward and uncomfortable position. But the embarrassing question which the Open University in turn poses for the whole of British higher education would still be there, even if the o u had not been brought into existence. The basic question is: Can a democratic industrial society spend as much money per year on a university student as it spends on paying an industrial worker— and at the same time satisfy the steadily increasing demand for higher education?

Planning: strategy and tactics

The Open University Planning Committee included representation from all areas of higher and further education, and from the b b c, from educational technology, and so on. It was thus not only a politically effective committee, but one which was well informed about the strategic considerations. For instance, in the case of broadcasting, it avoided many of the painful mistakes which had been made, and are still being made, elsewhere (see Hooper, p. 178).

The senior BBC personnel who were responsible for Open University broadcasts were probably more fully aware of the problems in their own area than were any of the senior people in the other main specialized areas. The BBC appears to have been right in its decision to recruit young academics and train them in production; this common background in specialized academic expertise has enabled relations between Open University and BBC personnel to be more cordial than most people expected. However, although these arrangements make possible the close integration between BBC broadcasts and the other teaching materials, this integration has often not occurred in the early courses; for example, material from broadcasts seldom seems to get into students' essays.

The detailed arrangements for the regional structure, for counselling, face-to-face teaching and assignment marking, all had to be worked out in 1970. In the early days it was not realized that by 1973 there would be nearly 500 full-time employees in the regional offices. Whereas the staff at the centre are at least working within quite well thought out strategic guidelines, the regional offices are much more the result of improvisation. Staff in the regional offices are often frustratingly remote from both the students they are serving and the 'centre' at Walton Hall. Some activities carried out in regional offices— for instance the recruitment of part-time course tutors—might be more efficiently done from the centre.

The new division of labour

Any innovatory organization invents new sorts of jobs. Some have deceptively familiar titles. The Open University has 'lecturers', but these people do not lecture—instead they write courses, edit readers, set exams, and make broadcasts (see Salaman and Thompson, p. 120). Other OU job titles are relatively unfamiliar in a university setting: Photographic Manager, Copyrights Manager, Director of Marketing, Manager of Correspondence Services, Chief Systems Analyst, Project Control Officer.

The thousands of part-timers employed by the OU find themselves in roles in some ways similar to those of extra-mural teachers or teaching assistants within an ordinary university. It is true that teaching by graduate students is common within most American and British universities. But the Open University 'course tutor' is unlike an American teaching assistant in that the latter is normally a graduate student in the same university, and thus himself part of the system. O U course tutors have a more demanding job (and are usually better qualified for it) because not only are they part-time teachers but they are outsiders to a system which on the one hand provides all the materials in considerable detail, but which on the other hand badly needs the spark which face-to-face teaching alone can provide for at least some students. Part-timers also carry the main burden of assessing students' work and in marking examination essays.

Some paradoxes, problems and dilemmas

One of the most serious problems of the O U is its casualties. 'Casualties' may seem a hard word for the thousands of students who fail to complete their courses; however I suspect that many students who have been encouraged, or have encouraged themselves, to think that they are not educational failures, but then do indeed fail the O U courses, must often experience a double sense of failure. Sometimes—for instance, if the student's own children are at the same time passing *their* exams—this must be especially humiliating. Some students who manage to 'keep going' only do so as the result of quite extraordinary self-sacrifice and determination.

Inequalities between one O U student and another tend to be greater than between students elsewhere; moreover the operation of the O U system tends to magnify these major existing inequalities. Not only are there unequal financial and educational backgrounds, but also major differences in age and in family, work, and other commitments. Inequalities are further magnified by the optional nature of Local Education Authority grants for O U students; and this fact once again falls unequally upon students in different faculties.

The comparison between science or technology students and those in arts or social sciences poses other dilemmas. Open University science, technology and maths staffing is being rapidly increased; science courses involve expensive experimental kits;

they require the employment of technicians, and these courses use much more of the expensive resource of television. In addition, science, technology and maths attract fewer students. Thus despite its general cost advantages the Open University cannot automatically assume that its science and technology graduates will be produced more cheaply than those produced elsewhere—especially in polytechnics. Scientists and technologists in polytechnics and in other universities are naturally sceptical, and will presumably remain so, until figures become available which separate out the costs of degrees obtained within different OU faculties.

Other problems arise from the OU's abolition of the lecture. While this raises the important question for all universities of what lectures are supposed to be doing, at least some OU students are hungry for at least some lectures. The regional arrangements of the Open University obviously provide many difficulties. One suggestion is that some regional operations could be transferred to the centre; there is also a, not necessarily inconsistent, suggestion for more and smaller regions. In the meanwhile, many students think that the OU is not fully aware of their problems.

In contrast to the frustration and difficulties of many students the complaints of the central academic staff may seem petty. The major complaint focuses on the excessive workload and the absence of time for research. University teachers normally expect, and are normally expected, to conduct research, and if this fails to happen the Open University will indeed not deserve the title 'University'.

More dilemmas: how large? which media?

Two of the most difficult questions during the middle and late 1970s will be the total number of students and the broadcasts. On numbers: If the OU is a radically cheaper way of producing graduates than has hitherto been found in Britain, is it right to restrict OU students to 'independent learning' adults following degree courses? If these benefits which follow from the economies of scale are so manifest, then what about non-degree students, eighteen-year-olds, and students already enrolled in other educational organizations?

Less strategically important, but even more complex are the dilemmas which surround the future of current ou broadcasting arrangements with the BBC. Early evening and week-end broadcasting hours are already becoming inadequate; and with the inexorable trend towards more and more hours of television the BBC may well be reluctant to cede so many hours on its second TV channel to the ou. This situation of rapidly increasing ou demand and probable decreasing BBC supply means that the ou's only chance of satisfactory hours must lie in some radical change.

The most obvious hope for the ou is that a fourth TV channel and a complete radio channel will, from 1976 onwards, be reserved for educational broadcasting. It is, however, by no means self-evident even if national educational radio and TV channels existed, that the Open University should get the lion's share of the week-ends and the week-day evenings. But while the 'old' electronic media of radio and through-the-air television present severe difficulties, none of the much vaunted 'new' electronic media seem likely to be nationally available in Britain (or any other country) at realistic cost—at least during the 1970s. The great bulk of current ou broadcasting costs are *production* costs (see Bates, p. 170); thus to be a practical possibility any kind of domestic video-playback device would need to be much cheaper than any of the current systems seems likely to be in either the 1970s or 1980s. In the long run, cable television appears to offer the best solution, but a system of cable TV throughout Britain would probably cost several thousand million pounds— and in the British context would have to rely on a Post Office initiative.

During the 1976–85 decade the ou may well be forced to settle for one of, or a combination of, several unsatisfactory solutions: dropping repeat broadcasts; using unpopular very early morning hours; relying heavily on sound tape-recordings and records; or running courses without any video or audio element.

The end of the beginning

The first two years of Open University teaching, 1971 and 1972, were devoted to undergraduate courses at foundation and second 'level'. But even in 1972 plans were already advanced for launching out well beyond these adult first degree students:

About 100 postgraduate part-time adult students began work in 1972; the first of five post-experience courses for 1973 began in January; some small schemes have started by which other educational organizations (such as a College of Education and the British Forces in Cyprus) adopt whole Open University courses for their students; the ou has also agreed to admit 500 eighteen-to twenty-one-year-olds to start courses in 1974. All these developments could, by the end of the 1970s, involve nearly as many students as the total number of undergraduate adult students (even if the number of the latter is enlarged).

This book is only an interim report on the early phase of the Open University. It is also a completely unofficial report—and the manuscript has deliberately not been shown to any senior officer of the university. In a few years' time there will doubtless be more authoritative and more weighty books than this one.

Jeremy Tunstall

Part I

Interim history

Chapter 1

An interim history of the Open University

Brian MacArthur

Editor, The Times Higher Education Supplement

The Open University was conceived on Easter Sunday, 1963, in the Scilly Islands home of Harold Wilson, newly-elected Leader of the Labour Opposition. All through the following seven years, in spite of his other preoccupations in Government, he remained loyal to the idea of the University of the Air which he sketched out on paper in his study that morning after church; often, indeed, he intervened unobtrusively on the university's behalf in the difficult arguments that occurred in Whitehall, especially with the Treasury.

The idea of a university of the air had undoubtedly been forming in other minds before it was put into a major speech by Mr Wilson. A wireless university was mooted within the BBC by Mr J. C. Stobart in 1926, the idea occurred to Sir George Catlin in 1946, the ITA published a pamphlet by Professor George Wedell on it in 1961, which was passed on to Mr Wilson, and Dr Michael Young, head of Labour Party research, wrote an article on an 'Open University' in 1962. The BBC and the Ministry of Education were also considering plans for a College of the Air. Mr Wilson, however, has no recollection now that anybody had put a proposal to him. The idea of the university had been forming in his mind both as a result of his friendship with Senator William Benton, Chairman of *Encyclopedia Britannica*, and from his frequent visits to the Soviet Union, and he was working on a plan for the university before he became leader. He had discovered, for instance, that 60 per cent of Soviet engineering graduates got their degrees after a correspondence course, combined with tuition by radio, followed by a year at university in Leningrad or Moscow. He was also interested in visual aids and on his annual visit to Chicago in January 1963 he asked Senator Benton (who was to become a benefactor of the Open University) if he could see some of the teaching films marketed by *Encyclopedia Britannica* for the Chicago College of the Air. Hugh Gaitskell, leader of the Labour Party, died while Mr Wilson was in Chicago; but after his election as leader, Mr Wilson continued working quietly on a means of reconciling the methods of the Soviet Union with the aids to teaching put out by *Encyclopedia Britannica* so that both could be used in Britain.

It was not until later in 1963 that he saw an opportunity of putting his idea across in a major speech. On 8 September Mr Wilson was due to launch the pre-election campaign of the Scottish Labour Party. He knew that his speech would not be reported outside Scotland if he concentrated solely on Scottish affairs, so he inserted a section about the University of the Air. On Monday, *The Times* carried a detailed account of his speech and there was also a commentary in *The Economist*. Speaking to a capacity audience in Glasgow, Mr Wilson said that the Labour Party was working on plans for a University of the Air and nationally-organized correspondence courses. A state-aided project of this kind might be presented on the fourth television channel. According to the report in *The Times*, his proposals were for the provision of facilities for home study up to university and higher technical standards.

At this early stage, it is clear that the 'university' which Mr Wilson outlined was not the authentic university, with its own charter, genuine academic standards and autonomy, that emerged at the later insistence of Miss Jennie Lee, who was determined that it should not be, as she continually declared, 'Paddy, the next best thing'. The university as he outlined it was a rational re-ordering of the facilities of the existing agencies of adult education—university extra-mural departments, the Workers' Education Association, the further education work of the BBC, correspondence colleges such as Wolsey Hall, and local night classes. Nor was there any mention that it was to be a university to redeem the failure of the traditional universities to recruit more than a small proportion of their students from working class homes.

A year later in 1964 the University of the Air appeared in the Labour manifesto for the general election, and when a Labour Government was returned Jennie Lee was appointed Minister of Arts in the Ministry of Public Building and Works. One of the early aims of Mr Wilson, now prime minister, was to remove responsibility for the arts from the Treasury. He succeeded when Miss Lee, her Ministry and her budget were transferred to the Department of Education and Science in 1965, when she was also given responsibility for the University of the Air. This was the fateful, crucial decision in the early history of the university. Mr Wilson knew that by selecting Jennie Lee to steer it into being he had chosen a politician of steely, imperious will, coupled both with tenacity and charm, who was no respecter of protocol and who would refuse to be defeated or frustrated by the scepticism about the university which persisted not only in the Department of Education and Science but also in the universities, among MPs, and among the community of adult educators. It is universally agreed that the university became like a religion to her. Miss Lee dealt directly with the Prime Minister, who delegated responsibility for the university totally to her, which had the added advantage that she dealt directly with the Treasury. Over the next few years, before the commitment of the Government was made explicit, the Treasury often complained that Miss Lee was eroding the Government's formal position in her public statements and in the Commons, but her link with Downing Street enabled her to carry on regardless. At the same time, Mr Wilson, again showing his commitment to the university, asked the ubiquitous Lord Goodman, his personal solicitor (who was then still comparatively unknown to the general public) to advise Miss Lee. It was he who conducted the early negotiations with the BBC.

Jennie Lee visited both Moscow and Chicago. Over the next few years she also used her charm on many of the most influential figures in and around Whitehall or the university establishment; among them Sir William Armstrong, head of the home civil service, who was sympathetic; Lord Goodman, Lord Robbins, Sir Eric Ashby, soon to be vice-chancellor of Cambridge University, Lord Fulton, vice-chancellor of Sussex University. and Professor Roy Shaw, who helped to dispel the suspicions about the university of the university extra-mural movement. The idea of using a fourth channel for education had been mooted since the early sixties. Yet the inspectorate, speaking for the Ministry of Education, told the Pilkington Committee on broadcasting that there was no educational case for a separate television channel. Their view was challenged and changed by administrative civil servants in the Ministry. Steps were taken to establish close links with the BBC, whose controller of Educational Broadcasting, Mr John Scupham, eventually played a critical role in the establishment of the Open University. A first scheme for a dawn to dusk, nursery to university, regional educational service, using the BBC, failed to get off the ground but by 1965 a detailed scheme for a College of the Air, with a role in further, adult, and refresher education, was ready for submission to Ministers. Among those who had worked on it at weekly dinners at the BBC were Mr Scupham, his successor, Mr Richmond Postgate, and Mr Cyril English, Mr Harry French, members of the Inspectorate, and Mr Ralph Toomey, a senior civil servant from the Department of Education and Science.

Jennie Lee started in her first week as she went on in the next five years—with an early display of her will and her determination that she would not be frustrated in establishing a university and nothing but a university.

On her fourth day at the Department, Miss Lee scrapped the College, emphasizing that she wanted a university, awarding degrees and making no compromise on academic standards. The idea of the college was never raised again. What motivated her insistence on a university (which clearly limited the potential of reaching a mass audience by television and radio) can only be guessed at. The most common suggestion is that she saw the university as an abiding memorial to Aneurin Bevan, a graduate of the National Labour College, offering a university education to those (like him) who were deprived of it, mainly by their social background, earlier in their lives. Only the very best, therefore, was good enough. As the White Paper on A University of the Air was to say in February 1966: 'There can be no question of offering to students a makeshift project inferior in quality to other universities. That would defeat its whole purpose. Its status will be determined by the quality of its teaching.' She also knew that adult education was the Cinderella of the DES—'the patch on the backside of the trousers'—and that it would be dangerous if the university, by any suggested association with the adult education movement, was tainted with the same image.

At this stage, the development of the project moved to the setting up of an advisory committee, although early negotiations were also started with the BBC. The membership of the advisory committee was especially distinguished by its expertise in the technology of education, but still lacked the support of the university establishment that was to emerge only when the Planning Committee was established, and then only grudgingly. Under the chairmanship of Miss Lee, the members were:

Professor K. J. Alexander, Professor of Economics, University of Strathclyde

Lord Annan, Provost, King's College, Cambridge

Dr E. W. Briault, Deputy Education Officer, Inner London Education Authority

Dr Brynmor Jones, Vice-Chancellor of the University of Hull

Mr D. J. G. Holroyde, Director, University of Leeds Television Centre

Mr Peter Laslett, Fellow of Trinity College, Cambridge

Mr N. I. Mackenzie, Director of the Centre for Educational Technology, University of Sussex

Mr A. D. Peterson, Director, Department of Education, University of Oxford

Dr O. G. Pickard, Principal, Ealing Technical College

Professor F. Llewellyn-Jones, Principal, University College of Swansea

Mr J. Scupham, Retired Controller of Educational Broadcasting, British Broadcasting Corporation

Professor H. Wiltshire, Professor of Adult Education, University of Nottingham.

Miss Lee drove the Committee hard and it reported quickly, a month before the 1966 general election—but still without any explicit commitment by the Government to the foundation of the university. The crucial sentence was: 'The government believe that by an imaginative use of new teaching techniques and teacher/student relationships, an open university providing degree courses as rigorous and demanding as those in existing universities *can* be established.' As will be noticed, it did not say 'will be' but 'can be'. This was also the first occasion on which the eventual description of the university was mentioned. The preamble said:

In the educational world, as elsewhere, technological discoveries are making a profound impact. Television and radio, programmed learning and a wide range of audio-visual aids have already brought about considerable changes. The most important, undoubtedly, is that the best of our teachers can now be made available to vastly wider audiences. A distinguished lecture that at one time might have been heard only by a handful of students, or a few hundreds at most, can now be broadcast to millions of listeners. It has, therefore, become possible for the first time to think in terms of a University of the Air.

A substantial network of educational institutions provide higher and further education for both full-time and part-time students. But opportunities can be still further enlarged to meet the needs of many not attracted by traditional institutions or unable for a variety of reasons, to take advantage of them.

The Government believe that by an imaginative use of new teaching techniques and teacher/student relationships, an open university providing degree courses as rigorous and demanding as those in existing universities can be established.

Its purpose will be three-fold. It will contribute to the improvement of educational, cultural and professional standards generally by making available to all who care to look and listen, scholarship of a high order.

Secondly, a minority of those showing general interest will want to accept the full disciplines of study and make use of all the facilities offered. These students will be enabled to acquire degrees and other qualifications as described in the Report of the Advisory Committee that follows.

Thirdly, it will have much to contribute to students in many other parts of the world as well as those studying in the United Kingdom. In the developing countries in particular, there is an urgent need not only for elementary education but for a highly trained corps of men and women, equipped to provide leadership in national life.

From the outset it must be made clear that there can be no question of offering to students a make-shift project inferior in quality to other universities. That would defeat its whole purpose, as its status will be determined by the quality of its teaching.

Its aim will be to provide, in addition to television and radio lectures, correspondence courses of a quality unsurpassed anywhere in the world. These will be reinforced by residential courses and tutorials.

At a time when scarce capital resources must, in the national interest, be allocated with the greatest prudence, an open university could provide higher and further education for those unable to take advantage of courses in existing colleges and universities. And it could do so without requiring vast capital sums to be spent on bricks and mortar.

Nor would its courses conflict in any way with teaching now provided in W.E.A. and other adult education centres, colleges of further education or on B.B.C. and I.T.A. educational programmes. On the contrary, those who left school at an early stage would have an added incentive to equip themselves by such means for higher study.

The White Paper also considered the sort of degrees the university should offer (which were to be general, without honours, based on two majors and three minors), the supporting services and agencies it might use, an organizational framework, including a vice-chancellor, and suggested that the university should be under the DES rather than the University Grants Committee.

Until the university started teaching in January 1971, its supporters could never be certain that it would be founded and there were two periods of serious uncertainty. One occurred now, immediately after the 1966 election, when the full rigour of the economic crisis hit the Government. There was still no commitment to the university on the part of the Government; Mr Crosland, Secretary of State for Education and Science, was probably agnostic about the project, the Cabinet was not universally enthusiastic, civil servants were sceptical, and it was an obvious candidate in the search for economies in public expenditure. Yet somehow it survived, probably chiefly because it had the support of the Prime Minister. Answering questions in the Commons, Jennie Lee constantly said that it was going ahead. Yet at one stage she was so despondent that she asked Sir John (now Lord) Fulton, vice-chancellor of Sussex University, and his colleague, Mr Norman Mackenzie, director of its Centre for Educational Technology (a member of her advisory committee and a friend since his *New Statesman* days), to dinner in London. She put to them a proposal to set up the university at Brighton, suggesting that Sussex should change its charter so that it could award external degrees to students of the Open University. After consideration, Sir John suggested that Sussex might be willing to join in a scheme based on a consortium of universities.

The climate of crisis passed, however, and the task now was to find a chairman for the planning of the university. If the scepticism of the establishment was to be overcome, it was essential that the chairman should have the respect of the academic world. An early choice was Sir Peter Venables, who deliberated for a weekend and then accepted. This was the second fateful decision in the development of the university. Apart from being vice-chancellor of Aston University, Sir Peter was deputy-chairman of the Committee of Vice-chancellors and Principals. Aston was a former college of advanced technology and he was chairman of the Further Education Advisory Committee of the BBC, as well as being on the Adult Education Committee of the Independent Television Authority. He was an establishment figure with the right blend of credentials, neither crusty nor over radical, with experience on both sides of the university plimsoll line, and a knowledge of broadcasting.

As he deliberated over the weekend, Sir Peter asked himself whether the university was simply a political gimmick or whether it had genuine potential. Several calculations convinced him of its potential. He drew a curve, for instance, of the expansion of further and higher education since 1938, when only 1·5 per cent of eighteen-year-olds went into universities. Nearly one and a half million adults, he estimated, had made only one mistake; they were born too early. If only 10 per cent of them seized the opportunity of a second chance the university was in business, added to which there were 300,000 non-graduate teachers with a strong motivation to work for the degrees which would increase their salaries and pensions. Social inequalities and late motivation, moreover, would not vanish with the establishment of the university—these would be a substantially continuing task. Another appeal, he thought, would be in the provision of post-experience courses, aimed to help men and women at critical stages of their careers. Another factor was his feeling that an Open University could be a means of liberating knowledge for the masses using the mass media, and he had a long involvement with technical and adult education.

The planning committee had been constituted before Sir Peter was appointed but Jennie Lee had succeeded in recruiting a membership which could not politically be ignored. Its members represented the leadership of every influential sector of educational opinion vital to the creation of the university, and included five members of the original advisory committee (John Scupham, Dr E. Briault, Dr Brynmor Jones, Mr N. Mackenzie and Professor H. Wiltshire).

There were five university vice-chancellors, three adult education professors, the principal of a leading polytechnic, two important leaders of education authorities and a sprinkling of well-known academics. The full membership was:

Sir Peter Venables, Chairman (Vice-Chancellor of the University of Aston in Birmingham)

Sir William Alexander (General Secretary of the Association of Education Committees)

Sir Eric Ashby (Vice-Chancellor of the University of Cambridge)

Dr E. W. H. Briault (Deputy Education Officer of the Inner London Education Authority)

Professor Asa Briggs (Vice-Chancellor of the University of Sussex)

Lord Fulton (former Vice-Chancellor of the University of Sussex)

Lord Goodman (Solicitor; Company Director; Fellow of University College London; Chairman of the Arts Council)

Mr Brian Groombridge (Education Officer, Independent Television Authority)

Professor Hilde T. Himmelweit (Professor of Social Psychology, London School of Economics)

Mr I. Hughes (Warden of Coleg Harlech)

Sir Brynmor Jones (Vice-Chancellor of the University of Hull)

Dr F. J. Llewellyn (Vice-Chancellor of the University of Exeter)

Mr Norman Mackenzie (Director of the Centre for Educational Technology at the University of Sussex)

Mr Roderick Maclean (Director of the University of Glasgow Television Service)

Dr A. J. Richmond (Principal of Lanchester College of Technology)

Professor Lord Ritchie-Calder (University of Edinburgh)

Mr J. Scupham (former Controller of BBC Educational Broadcasting)

Professor Roy Shaw (Director of Adult Education, University of Keele)

Professor Harold Wiltshire (Professor of Adult Education, University of Nottingham).

One other factor was crucial in forming the attitude of Sir Peter as chairman. He reckoned that speed was now all important and that the Government could not afford a showdown. He knew that he could stand out for his view of the university and of its rights as a university. The insistence of Jennie Lee that her creation should be a university, with no taint of the second-rate, was now re-inforced by a chairman of equally determined character who ensured that a university with traditional British university autonomy was created.

A month before the first meeting of the Planning Committee, Jennie Lee called a London press conference, which showed that after four years the concept of the university was evolving more closely to the final model, leaving the committee only to put academic flesh to the skeleton created behind the scenes.

The most significant announcement was that the television programmes would be provided on BBC 2, an agreement which had been achieved only after tough bargaining with—and within—the BBC. After the publication of the White Paper, the Government approached the BBC and the ITA about the establishment of a fourth television channel for the university. On investigation it was shown that it would cost at least £25m, which could not be afforded, and Lord Goodman, on behalf of the Government, then discussed arrangements with the BBC for using BBC 2 and radio for the university. It was eventually agreed in March 1966 that the BBC would offer ten hours of television time in the first year of the university's operation, rising to thirty hours in the third, on BBC 2. It was also understood that the broadcasts would occur in the early evening until 7.30, eventually going on until 8. A year later, however, the introduction of colour on b b c 2 led to a reappraisal of programme timings. Added to this, the b b c had also told the university that it saw no solution to the provision of radio programmes, except by creating a new and expensive v h f system or using local radio. As soon as the Planning Committee was formed, Sir Peter wrote to the b b c protesting that its offer would diminish the value and impact of the university's programmes, just when it needed to make a strong initial impression. A strong streak of scepticism about the university persisted within the b b c. Sir Hugh Greene, the director-general, may have shared it, but his political sense told him that if the university was going to be created, the b b c must be involved in it. After hard bargaining an agreement was eventually reached, and appeared as Appendix I in the report of the Planning Committee. It emphasized that the university and b b c staff would work as an 'educational partnership' under which each had a specific role to play, over the whole range from the conception of the course to the final production of the programmes.

There were two early and crucial decisions in the Planning Committee. At the suggestion of Roderick Maclean it was decided to adopt a January–December academic year (which meant that the summer vacation could be used for summer schools). And at the suggestion of Norman Mackenzie it was decided to opt for a system of course credits. Working groups were set up to study ways and means, students and curriculum (under Professor Asa Briggs) and constitution and organization.

The final report was sent to Edward Short, Secretary of State for Education and Science, on 31 December 1968, only fourteen months after the Committee first met. Mr Short had been the firmest supporter of Jennie Lee in ministerial committees in the early days of the Labour Government and he was the first education minister of the Government to show any public enthusiasm for it. As soon as he received the Venables report, he speeded publication and, speaking in the Commons on 28 January 1969, he said the the Government 'fully accepted' the outlined plan of development set out. So, at last, there was a firm, explicit statement that the Government intended to go ahead. Mr Short had got the backing of the Cabinet, even though several ministers, notably Mr Richard Crossman, were sceptical of it. Mr Short added that it would now be for the university authority, 'as an independent and completely autonomous institution', to carry the project forward. It could count on the support of the Government. Although Sir Edward Boyle carefully steered a middle path during his period as Opposition education spokesman, never once saying that a Conservative Government would abolish the university, there was an immediate indication from him of the Opposition's scepticism. The proposal, he said, came forward at a time when resources for essential educational tasks were more stretched than in any year since the war. Did it make sense for Mr Short to commit himself to funds of the order of £3·7m a year, particularly as the Venables Report might suggest techniques and innovations that could be adopted more efficiently and less expensively by existing institutions providing part-time degree courses and other forms of adult education? The Opposition could not guarantee to spend at the same rate. All this underlined the political problem of getting the university into being that now confronted Dr Walter Perry, forty-six, the new vice-chancellor, and Mr Anastasios Christodoulu, thirty-six, secretary of the university.

Walter Perry was the third crucial personality in the development of the university. Selected from more than a hundred candidates, he was exactly the sort of candidate Sir Peter Venables —who insisted that the appointment should be made solely on academic grounds—was seeking: vice-principal of Edinburgh University, holder of the chair of pharmacology, convener of the committee which had recast the medical curriculum and introduced the new degree of B.Sc (medical sciences), a serious candidate for a university vice-chancellorship at any of the traditional universities. He and Mr Christodoulu now set about the task of establishing a university and a university of a sort that had never been created before, presenting unique academic and administrative problems—in the space of two years. Jennie Lee found the Open University offices of an opulent and palatial nature in Belgrave Square.

Just as vital as attracting the right vice-chancellor and secretary was the job of finding the right chancellor and treasurer. Lord Crowther, chairman of *The Economist*, became Chancellor and Sir Paul Chambers, chairman of Royal Insurance and a former chairman of ICI, became treasurer. Neither appointment was popular with some Government ministers, who felt that men at least of Labour sympathies should have been appointed, but Sir Peter Venables and Dr Perry insisted on the independence of the university to make its own appointments, free of any interference. They were supported by Jennie Lee, who insisted to her colleagues that the university was not going to be an 'educational ghetto', a Labour university for the proletariat.

Walter Perry shared the philosophy of Jennie Lee about the university—that the most important task was to win the respect of its academic peers, the other universities, mainly so that it could attract academic staff as teachers and examiners, and establish the principle of academic interchangeability. He was no conservative academic and wanted the university to be more adventurous, less stereotyped and younger than the traditional universities—but he also wanted their respect. Social purpose was not paramount. He simply wanted to create a university open to anybody, with no entry qualifications, whose degrees were of the same standard as others.

Although the academic map of the university was now being charted—often single-handed by Walter Perry and Mr Christodoulu—Whitehall and Westminster still obtruded; a political campaign had still to be fought. A director of information was appointed at a professorial salary and newspaper education correspondents were subtly courted. The six senior officers of the university held regular dinners for influential guests, among them Sir William Armstrong, Sir William Pile, permanent secretary of the DES, Lady Plowden, Margaret Thatcher (after her appointment as shadow education spokesman) and Harold Wilson (when he returned to Opposition). The most important job, however, was to form some assessment of student numbers, to draw up estimates of costs, and to get a budget. Nobody knew how many potential students there were. The Planning Committee, however, had suggested that there might be 170,000 to 450,000 potential students, of whom between 34,000 to 150,000 might register with the university.

There were constant battles with the Treasury, as the costs of the university started to climb, in a period when Roy Jenkins, the chancellor, was determined to bring Britain into balance and to redeem the Government's record. Nor was there any indication at all that the Conservatives were becoming more sympathetic. Sir Peter Venables and Walter Perry had seen Sir Edward Boyle and Mr Richard Hornby before a debate in 1969, and Sir Edward had at least held to his non-committal policy, but Edward Heath had told the BBC that there could be no guarantee of survival for the university. The shadow chancellor, Iain Macleod, moreover, held to his view that the Open University was a 'nonsense'. Edward Short had several other priorities, apart from the Open University. He wanted to start a nursery school programme and he wanted to maintain the level of school building. He constantly scrutinized Open University costs, in an effort to keep them down, whilst fighting with the Chancellor of the Exchequer on the university's behalf. An effort by the Treasury to cut back the initial enrolment to 10,000 was resisted, both by Harold Wilson and Edward Short, and it was agreed that the university should enrol 25,000 students in each of the first three years. After the election, however, the university agreed, under duress, that the student population should level out at 36,000 to 42,000 instead of 55,000. The university, meanwhile, had forged ahead. As the election approached, acceptance offers had been made to students for admission in January 1971. Staff had been appointed, and university buildings were rising at a dramatic rate at Walton, near Milton Keynes.

The university heard of its first triennial vote in the last three days of the labour Government. Yet the vote was immediately put in doubt by the election of the Heath Government and it is said—and cannot be confirmed—that a paper proposing the abolition of the university was on the desk of Iain Macleod the night he died. The new Government also arrived with a commitment to cut public spending. A month later, the university's budget was cut by £1m over three years but the Government endorsed the university.

Mrs Thatcher, who shared the concern of the Labour Government about the flow of 'suitably qualified' entrants from school to conventional higher education, felt that the Open University should make some contribution to meeting the expansion of student numbers.

Some sections of the DES had certainly seen the Open University as a means of helping to solve the problems they confronted in doubling student numbers in universities, polytechnics and colleges of education by 1982. There had been an insidious campaign to try to persuade the Minister that the Open University should be used for eighteen-year-olds, an obvious denial or, as some would put it, extension of its purpose—and possibly an unsuitable use of a teaching system designed essentially for adults—but a tempting method of expanding higher education more cheaply. Now that the Conservative Government was in power, they partly succeeded and the university told Mrs Thatcher that it was willing to examine urgently the extent to which it could admit school-leavers.

The university undoubtedly did not want to admit eighteen-year-olds, but Walter Perry and Sir Peter Venables were pragmatists. Governments come and go, but universities go on for ever; they probably felt that a small compromise which might lead to a small pilot experiment was worth making, not only as a delaying tactic but as a means of ensuring the survival of a university which is now the talk of the world. Mrs Thatcher succeeded in July 1972, but only after a long delay caused by the doubts of the university's Senate and Council. A pilot project that started out from the DES as an experiment with 5,000 eighteen-year-olds became an experiment with 500, of whom half were to be unqualified, which is due to start in 1974.

Two significant developments in 1973 finally heralded the fulfilment of the early ambitions of Dr Perry and Jennie Lee. The Committee of Vice-Chancellors and Principals of the United Kingdom invited Dr Perry to attend its meetings, a symbolic judgment by the university's 'conventional' peers that it was now a member of the 'club'.

The university also got its second triennial budget of £33·6m. It had wanted £39·4m. It had also wanted to expand its undergraduate population to 48,000 by 1976 but was told, disappointingly, that 42,000 was the upper limit. At least, however, its future was assured until the end of the seventies; and few doubted that it was now a permanent addition to Britain's higher education system.

Some—and they may be right—say that history will judge the National Health Service and the Open University as Britain's major achievements of the second half of the twentieth century. It would be pleasant to say that the Open University, like the health service, represented the triumph of an irresistible idea whose time had come. It was not. At any stage until the first students started work in January 1971, it could have been stifled by men without imagination—and nearly was.

Part II

Implications

Chapter 2

The economic implications

Leslie Wagner

Lecturer in Economics

Any new institution competing with others for a limited amount of public funds must prove its cost-effectiveness. The Open University need have no fear on this account. Cost comparisons already made between the OU and conventional British universities (Wagner, 1972) indicate that on the basis of the first three years of operation it costs less than a third of other institutions to teach an equivalent undergraduate at the Open University. It is more difficult to be precise over the relative *cost per graduate*, but if the Open University drop-out rate was 50 per cent, the relative advantage would be the same. Indeed the drop-out rate at the Open University would have to rise to about 85 per cent for the cost per graduate at the two institutions to be the same.

Capital cost comparisons are even more significant. The capital cost per student place at the Open University is about 6 per cent of that at conventional universities. And this excludes residential costs. If the latter are included, the Open University's relative cost is about 3 per cent.

Finally there are the *resource costs*—the cost to the economy of allocating these resources to higher education. Besides the costs already mentioned, resource costs also include the immediate lost output to the economy.

With full-time students the economy forgoes the output which they might otherwise have produced. Full-time students at conventional universities probably cost the British economy some £200 million per annum in output forgone. The assumption is that their extra qualifications and ability as a result of higher education will increase output by far more than this in the long run.

The part-time OU student costs the economy very little in

forgone output and can be expected to make the same contribution to higher education in the future as the conventional university student. If the 35,000-plus students at the Open University were full-time instead of part-time, then, ignoring housewives and other non-earning students, it would cost the economy nearly £30 million per annum in output forgone. Because of this the resource cost of teaching an equivalent undergraduate at the Open University is about one-sixth of that at conventional universities. This figure does not include the cost of *maintenance grants* which the full-time student requires. These are not a resource cost but a money transfer from one group in the community (taxpayers) to another (students).

The Open University is likely to lose some of this cost advantage as it develops and makes available a wider range of courses. It has two alternatives. It can maintain the same staff numbers, allowing more courses to be produced as staff finish producing existing ones: this is likely to be a rather slow process since existing courses need to be revised every four years. Alternatively, the university can engage more staff to produce a larger number of courses more quickly, but this will entail higher costs. The objective will be to produce more courses for the same number of students rather than more courses as student numbers increase, which was the situation of the first three years.

The cost of producing a full credit course at the Open University, including broadcasting (which accounts for roughly half of this cost) is in the region of £150,000 to £250,000 depending on whether it is arts- or science-based. So a decision to produce (say) five extra courses per annum is likely, on present staff numbers, to cost the university about an extra £1 million per annum and to raise its budget by 10 per cent. However, an extra five courses per annum would be an increase of 50 per cent on the number of new courses introduced each year and would still leave the University with a comfortably large cost advantage. It should also be remembered that five extra courses per annum builds up to a substantial figure after a number of years.

How the cost advantage arises

One reason is the part-time nature of the students. The importance of this for the resource cost comparisons has already been mentioned. In addition the Robbins Committee argued that a part-time student costs half as much to teach as a full-time student. However, this view has been challenged by many concerned with education. It is probably only true where part-time students are a very small proportion of the total student population. In this situation they use existing buildings and other resources at a low marginal cost. In a higher educational institution with a large proportion of part-time students it is doubtful if the cost implications are significantly below those catering for full-time students.

Another element in the cost advantage of the Open University arises out of its method of production. The use of correspondence material and broadcasting imposes a high fixed cost to production, but allows substantial economies of scale as student numbers rise.

Consider the costs of teaching at a conventional university and then at O U, ignoring for the time being capital costs. The main cost element in the teaching process at conventional universities is the lecturer and there is an accepted ratio of students to teachers. Raise the number of students and you have to raise the number of teachers.

Most of the Open University's teaching costs are unrelated to the number of students. The teaching staff numbers are related more to the number of courses than to the number of students. And they are only one element in the teaching process. The preparation and production of a correspondence unit requires the work of the central academic staff, the media and publishing sections, and the printers. Once prepared and printed to a certain minimum number, it is only the cost of paper, ink and postage that increases as student numbers rise. The average cost per student falls dramatically as more students receive the material.

This situation is even more apparent with broadcasting costs. One 24-minute O U television programme costs on average about £4,000 to make. This cost stays the same whether 10 or 10,000 students watch the programme.

The Open University system is specifically geared to mass higher education. If used at a conventional British university where even standardized first-year courses rarely enrol more than a few hundred students, it would prove prohibitively expensive. There are, of course, elements in the O U teaching system which do vary with the number of students and these are the part-time tuition staff and certain elements of the cost of general regional services. These are small compared to major costs of tuition previously mentioned and it is estimated that an extra student at the Open University involves extra costs of close to £100 annually. In the conventional institutions an extra student is likely to involve about an extra £300 per year in teaching costs alone ignoring accommodation, catering and social requirements.

The low extra cost of increasing student numbers at the Open University means that the total student numbers expected in 1973 of about 38,000 do not fully exploit the economies of scale arising out of the production method. The average cost per student would continue to fall as student numbers rose and the latter could reach 70,000 before the main cost advantages of the system were being used.

The third area of advantage for the Open University is that its students live at home. Two distinctions need to be made here. Many conventional university students live away from home and require accommodation to be provided for them. The residential costs at a conventional university are in the region of £3,000 per three-year student place. But even those that *live* at home *study* elsewhere. The ou student lives and studies at home and it is because of this that the Open University establishes a large cost advantage.

A conventional university must provide teaching accommodation, laboratories, libraries, catering and recreational facilities for its students. All these involve large items of capital cost. The Open University provides none of these facilities as a capital item. A large proportion of teaching takes place in the student's home. In place of laboratories the science student carries out experiments in his own home and spends some time using the laboratories of existing institutions of higher education. This last element is an important one. A number of facilities are provided by using the spare capacity which already exists in the conventional system, at a very low marginal cost. For example, students use their home town library and where specialized papers are required, these are provided through off-prints. Catering and social provision are also met by using existing facilities.

By using existing capacity within the educational system and providing certain capital items as current materials, the Open

C. l

University produces an efficient method of tuition. Students may feel disadvantaged by not having as great an access to as wide a range of equipment or books as their colleagues in conventional institutions. But with programmed courses the materials they receive are tailored to their requirements.

Implications and policy suggestions

The nature of the Open University's cost advantage over conventional universities leads to a number of implications. First is the relative cheapness of increasing the number of students at the OU. Student numbers could *double* from their 1973 level of 38,000 and the effect would be to raise total costs by less than half.

The OU system arose out of the need to find a method that would allow part-time adult students to return to education with minimum disturbance to their present way of life. It has developed into a most efficient vehicle for mass higher education. Open University student numbers should be increased to allow the excess demand which has been apparent in its first three years of operation to be catered for.

But if the Open University can take extra students at a low marginal cost why should these students be restricted to adult, unqualified, part-timers? An institution of higher education which can provide an average of three times as many places per £ spent as conventional institutions is obviously very attractive to a government faced with an increasing demand for full-time higher education.

However, an attempt to alter the Open University's function, so that it might make a contribution to the demand for full-time higher education by school-leavers, is likely to cause it to lose some of its cost advantage. The OU operation is geared to part-time students—from the amount of work required in a week to the use of spare capacity in existing institutions at evenings and week-ends. To adapt the system to cater for full-time students would lose some of the cost advantages previously outlined.

The distinction between unqualified and qualified students would increase costs. Open University courses are designed particularly at foundation level for unqualified students who have spent some time away from formal education. The adaptations which would be necessary to cater for those who have been in the education system during the previous three years would add to the costs of the operation.

Any plan to make the university take eighteen-year-olds is likely to reduce the cost advantage and change its original concept. In making a contribution to reducing the excess demand for full-time higher education by qualified school-leavers, the university would be reducing the contribution it made to meeting the excess demand for part-time higher education by unqualified mature students which was its original function.

An alternative suggestion is that the Open University should be linked in some way with conventional universities, possibly by all students taking a common first year at the OU. This does not run into the cost disadvantages of the previous proposal and indeed exploits the most advantageous cost elements in the OU system. The major OU cost advantage is at foundation level, where a large number of students take a small number of courses and where the level of sophistication is not too high, so that the personal and more costly elements within the system can be utilized to greater effect.

The arguments against this proposal arise not out of their cost implications, but out of their damaging effect on the original and present functions of the Open University. The proposal implies that while the OU might be appropriate for unqualified mature students it is only capable of educating qualified school-leavers to first-year standard. The university is in effect a preparatory school for conventional universities. The effect this would have on staff recruitment and retention would soon make this a self-fulfilling prophecy. More important the whole scheme in its implied view of the academic standard of the OU would seriously devalue the status of the degree for part-time students.

The problem with attempting to integrate the Open University into the conventional system is that while it might well reduce the overall costs of higher education it will seriously damage the existing functions of the OU. One method of overcoming this would be to separate the OU from the system it uses. The OU should be allowed to continue catering for part-time unqualified mature students and should be allowed to expand its student numbers as explained earlier. The system it uses—correspondence material, broadcasts, a small element of personal tuition—should be embodied in a separate institution catering for full-time qualified school-leavers.

There are a number of alternatives within this basic framework. The separate institution could deal with all first-year students and might also cater for below degree standard courses and diplomas. More ambitiously, it could be a full university in its own right offering students an alternative method of obtaining a degree. The full-time institution—I have suggested elsewhere the possible title of the National University—might need to provide a greater range of personal tutorial services and greater access to libraries and laboratories. This would raise costs, but this could be offset by limiting entry to those students with access to major areas of population. Unlike the Open University, there is no necessity for this institution to be open. There is the present conventional alternative for students who cannot attend the new institution.

If the regional organization is fully equipped and efficiently operated, students should still be able to enjoy the cultural and social stimulation that many see as a major advantage of conventional universities. One other advantage of the proposal is that by studying full-time at home it may be possible to complete a degree in two years. As the system developed, some integration between National University and conventional university courses might be possible.

The important point about the economic implications of the Open University is that its cost advantage should not lead to developments which undermine its basic function. It is the system that the university uses which creates its cost advantage and it is the system, not the university, which should be adapted to meet the needs of full-time school-leavers. The Open University was established to meet a need. The fact that in meeting that need it devised an economic method of mass education should not be used to divert it from its original purpose.

Chapter 3

The seeds of radical change

Willem van der Eyken

Senior Research Fellow, Brunel University

The term most often applied to the Open University by those who observe it from the outside is 'innovative'. Nobody would deny that it is an apposite term, though there might be considerable argument about the exact nature of the innovations. The real point, however, is not the innovations themselves, but their effect upon Britain's established and slowly-evolving educational system; for they bring to that system certain concepts which are not only foreign, but to some extent, opposed to its accepted canons. The question I want to pose is simply this: What happens when you have a system with basically two internally inconsistent assumptions—its public face set towards mass higher education, with a private face bowing to the older, elitest traditions—and you introduce an element such as the Open University which exposes these contradictory assumptions, demonstrates their incompatibility to a pitch where they can no longer be ignored, and proffers some alternatives? You have, I believe, the seeds for radical change.

I want to consider only four provocative elements associated with the Open University. The first two occur in its very title—'open' and 'university'. No one, after all, talks of the 'open' primary school or the 'open' comprehensive, precisely because to do so would be tautological. It is the juxtaposition of an institution of higher education which imposes no prior academic achievement as a prerequisite for entry, next to a system that does just this, which makes the Open University so singular. What differentiates it is precisely the fact that it is 'open' to the extent that the rest of the system is 'closed'; a consumer-orientated element in a highly-selective product-orientated system. The word 'open' is, therefore, as much a comment of the education system as it is intended to describe one particular institution within it.

But how 'open' can the ou truly be? Some suggest that 'the major objective of the ou is to offer opportunities to educationally underprivileged groups' (Pratt, 1971) or that it was founded 'to mitigate social inequality' (Burgess, 1972). It is obvious that, outside the fevered rhetoric of politicians, no single educational institution can conduct social engineering on such a scale; in a selective system most of the 'selecting out' has been done by the age of eight, and certainly by sixteen. Moreover, no 'university' whose courses are based on the need for extensive reading of a highly concentrated kind, intensive effort over a very long period, commanding the facilities for peace and quiet, for receiving BBC 2 and VHF radio, for continuous paperwork and the considerable organizational ability to cope with more than thirty units of work a year, is in any position to appeal to the exhausted manual labourer with poor reading skills, uncomfortable with pen and paper (never mind a typewriter) and unused to textbooks.

That is not to say it cannot be 'open' at all. What it is able to do is to provide a genuine 'second chance' for all those who, for one reason or another, failed to get a first chance at a university education. That in itself is a considerable social service. Moreover, the rest of the system, being selective, ensures that it will have a continuing pool of applicants. Secondly, the ou makes available an 'open access' system of *education permanente* for those whose work needs constant up-dating. But beyond this, we run into the second question provoked by the Open University.

That is the relationship this 'university' is to have with those more traditional institutions offering three-year full-time undergraduate courses. If, as is now the case, eighteen-year-olds may enrol for its courses, we then have the curious situation in which youngsters are prevented, by their shortfall in 'A' levels, or their inability to achieve the right combination of GCE certificates, from entering a traditional university, but may with exactly the same background, work towards an ou degree. Given that the two forms of degree are equivalent in intellectual content, then this situation simply places in question the Robbins Committee's basis of two 'A' levels for entry to higher education; that is to say, the selective part of the system is shown to be in direct contradiction with the 'open' part of the system. We may then question the meaning of the word 'university' in the English context. What, pray, is a university? The faint answer is: 'A degree-granting institution.' (Not true, anyway, for the CNAA awards degrees, but has no students.) From here we proceed to the next conundrum: 'What is a degree?', and here we run into a further contradiction with the existing system, for whatever an OU degree might be, it is plainly not the same kind of thing as a degree from a conventional university.

In the first place, I believe that a student who works his way through six or eight courses of a full OU degree, in terms of sheer work, has covered extensively more ground than his conventional counterpart. (I speak feelingly, as one who has wrestled with the mathematics Foundation Course.) Consider the load. So far as we can judge, each course involves something like 30 to 34 units of work. Each unit consists of forty or more pages of sheer writing. Each unit is usually accompanied by a self-assessment battery, by a tutor-marked assignment, accompanying television and radio programmes, as well as by tutorial or counselling sessions, not to mention summer schools. Six of these courses qualify for a pass degree, eight for an honours degree. Excluding exemptions, the ordinary graduate will have waded through something like 180 units of work, not to mention the terminal examinations and summer schools.

I consider that his work-load is greater than that which is demanded of the ordinary university undergraduate. What it does not offer, of course, is the traditional quality of undergraduate life; the association with 'a community of scholars' and the social life amongst one's peers, the varied opportunities to extend one's leisure interests, the chance to broaden horizons among the multifarious student clubs. Correspondence courses, by their nature, are very much a 'nose-to-grindstone' business. The question here is—how important are these other, Newmanesque, elements, and how high do we rate them in our scales of values, as priorities begging for government funds? The Open University faces us with the actual uncomfortable opportunity to choose whether we want more people to be able to take degrees, or, for the same money, whether less shall do so but in doing so, enjoy the experience of 'going to university'.

This links with the third provocative factor about the Open University—its costs. The evidence here, as presented by Leslie Wagner (1972) is, to use his own words, that 'the gap between the Open University and the conventional universities' figures is too large to be ignored,' His analysis makes three points. The average recurrent cost per equivalent undergraduate place in the OU is about one-quarter of that in a traditional university. The capital cost per student is only about 6 per cent of what it is in a conventional university. Finally, the 'resource' cost—that is, the money spent on teaching and research, on the use of existing buildings, on putting up new buildings and the sums tied up in 'forgone earnings' by students—amounts to about one-sixth of that in a traditional university. Simply put, the Open University is just very much cheaper than the traditional system; so much cheaper, in fact, that it almost forces a policy decision down one's throat. Moreover, given the initial investment, the economies of scale will allow the OU to reduce its *per capita* costs very much further. Current calculations are based on a stable student population of about 40,000. But having produced the correspondence texts, made the television programmes and processed the radio tapes, there is no reason why the audience could not be increased considerably, to bring down the individual cost per student dramatically. Wagner, himself, believes that a ceiling might not be reached until the OU has a stable student population of some 60,000—that is, nearly twice as large as it is now.

The fourth factor which affects the entire system of higher education is the OU's teaching methods. I do not, here, want to stress the television and radio side, for I believe that these are very much overrated elements which, nevertheless, have amply demonstrated the need for yet another policy decision—the provision of a separate educational television channel. It is interesting that of the £250,000 it cost to develop the mathematics Foundation Course, half of the total expense went on this audio-visual aspect which many students, including myself, found the most dispensable part of the course. No, the important feature of the Open University's teaching methodology is the Correspondence Texts, and the most important feature of this is simply that it is available for all to see. In a word, 'open'.

This innovation in British practice is breathtaking in its audacity. It is one of the canons of national education that a teacher is not only master in his own class, but that it is understood that he will perform his function unmonitored, unwitnessed even, by a single other colleague. Headmasters and headmistresses know that they are helpless before this inalienable professional right. And these are people who have been 'trained' to teach! What of that army of totally untutored, unqualified, amateur lecturers who man the universities? They suddenly find themselves confronted with an entire library of structured, pre-tested course material almost certainly—because it has been edited, sent out on trials and through many hands—better than their own vague, rambling, unplanned and often unheard lec-tures. Not only is the comparison painful, but it is open for any student to make for himself.

What do these four facets of the Open University—its ready access, its definition of a university course, its low cost per place and its teaching methods—what do these things imply for the higher education system as a whole? One can, of course, only guess at all the implications, but there are a few straws in the wind. The Department of Education and Science has already embarked on a determined policy to siphon some of the present demand for university places to the polytechnic sector, to try and give its binary policy at last some semblance of credibility. At the same time, it is cutting the UGC target figure of 320,000 under-graduate places by 1976 down to about 305,000. It is already eroding the traditional ideal of university life by encouraging more students to go to their local university, by marginally increasing the student : teacher ratio, all with the aim of improv-ing the so-called 'efficiency' of universities.

None of this is, of course, more than tinkering. Both policy-makers and administrators in education are, it must be remem-bered, heavily Oxbridge biased, and demonstrate a timidity of approach which is only matched by the arrogance of the univer-sity community itself in, for example, dismissing Mrs Shirley Williams's twelve-point programme for change. What the Open University does is to bring out before the public gaze the chal-lenges that face the administrators. The facts can no longer be hidden behind a smokescreen of documents and reports. We have the means to choose between mass higher education and selective higher education. We can go either way. If we decide to retain our selective system, we will have to be able to justify that decision with a great deal more conviction than is at present the case, and in the background, the Open University will forever be disproving the facts. But if we go for mass higher education, then the whole UGC empire, the quinquennium arrangement and all that it embraces, is threatened. The Open University will then have to take on the characteristics of a National University, a central resource centre servicing the entire field of higher education. It will mean that we will have to reconsider under-graduate provision in terms of this central resource. And that could mean, for future generations, that their first contact with higher education was through this correspondence course system rather than automatically going off to a residential university.

Whether we like it or not, in creating the Open University, we have made a major change in the whole structure of the British education system.

Chapter 4

A view from New England

Norman Birnbaum

Professor of Sociology, Amherst College, Massachusetts

The Open University cannot be said to lack a sense of its historical mission. Those whose labors are recorded in these pages (cabinet ministers, Planning Committee, academic and administrative staff, media specialists and—of course—the students) are far from reticent about the importance of the experiment. Perhaps not enough has been said about the economic dimensions of the enterprise, its potentiality for satisfying a considerable social demand, its contribution to a new educational technology. Perhaps—but not for want of trying. There may be other aspects of the project, however, which can heighten our appreciation of it. I wish to say something, if in brief compass, about these.

I will begin on a rather personal note. I lived and taught in the United Kingdom from 1953 to 1964 (at the London School of Economics and Nuffield College, Oxford; and subsequently taught at the University of Strasbourg). I recall the debate of the 1950s on university expansion (and that terrible phrase, 'more means worse', which is apparently now rather less terrifying), and the discussion—not all of it dispassionate—of the Robbins Report. More importantly, I recall the ways in which the publication in 1957 of Richard Hoggart's *The Uses of Literacy* and Raymond Williams's *Culture and Society* changed the prevalent conception of a politics of culture. When I visited Milton Keynes in 1972, I was struck by the utter familiarity of the rhetoric of the Open University. The Open University is evidence that those who advocated an expansive, a morally generous notion of the politics of culture, did not labor in vain. Their labors, in turn, did not begin *in vacuo*.

The tradition of adult education in Britain is old and deep; it is also ambiguous. It has roots in both radical democracy and a much more conservative ethic. The idea that only an educated citizenry can assume its responsibilities for self-governance is different from the view that the nation's elites have the moral task of education. Both ideas co-exist in the Open University: a conception of cultural self-help, and a notion of cultural diffusion downward. Utopia is as yet remote; these views have not so fused as to have become indistinguishable. Not for the first time, the Labour Party has proven to be a more effective agent of what was once termed Tory Socialism than a Conservative Party caught between its supporters' privileges and a meritocratic ideology.

The Open University, then, is the legatee of a long sequence of attempts to make education a right. It is, no less emphatically, the most obvious heir of the British experience of adult education. Several generations of adult education explain the readiness of public authorities to lend it support, the enthusiasm of its full-time and part-time teachers, the students' grasp of its requirements. The actual educational genealogy of staff and students ought to be known. How many participated, or are offspring of those who did, in adult education? The idiom and logic of the institution would have been different under other historical conditions. The (justifiable) expectation that adult students, living off university premises, would want and could deal with academic subject matter is clearly connected with a national tradition.

The spiritual, as distinct from the technical, role of the BBC in the Open University is a somewhat different one. British public broadcasting has been marked by a pronouncedly paternalistic attitude to the diffusion of culture. If that attitude is now under severe revision, the BBC has long had a quasi-sacral cast. Where else in the world would one have found a 'Director of the Spoken Word'? If much of this is gone, the serious concern it reflected remains.

I have touched upon the willingness of the Open University's adult students to accept classical academic subject matter. The Open University is no experiment with what has emerged in America as the 'counter-culture'. It is not what we know as a University Without Walls, taking all the world as its classroom. Its pedagogic problem is not to help adolescents to grow by directing them to other life experiences, 'other' being defined as other than those available in typical middle class homes and schools. Its problem, indeed, is to take adults out of their life experiences in order to enable them to enter a rather different sphere of inquiry and thought. At first sight, its curriculum appears to ignore the past decade of university troubles. These troubles affected Britain less than the us or the continental countries, but they were certainly not entirely missing. They entailed a widespread criticism of the university curriculum, pervasive doubt amongst students (and not a few teachers) that traditional subject matter was worthwhile. I shall argue that first sight is very short, that the Open University may offer the beginnings of a solution to these questions.

For the moment, let it be said that the Open University profits from Britain's relative cultural homogeneity. Matthew Arnold would no doubt still find the country far too Philistine. He would admit, however, that the Barbarians have all but disappeared, and that the Populace has merged with the Philistines. No very great progress? The universities and the schools have leavened Philistinism to a considerable degree. Arnold would be most gratified that the Open University's adult students, to judge by their testimony, still believe that education consists in learning something very like the best that has been thought and said.

How may we explain the Open University's students' faith in the value of a university education? Possibly, they respect higher education (and culture in general) as possessions which mark the acquisition of true middle class standing. No one can read their testimony, however, without being moved by their vision of a larger life, a vision not reducible to the possibilities of changed careers. In them, the liberal idea of the autonomous development of the personality lives in its older form. The changes many of them seek in their own lives are changes of intellectual capacity, of viewpoint, of knowledge—changes they think they can make, even if all else in society stands still.

Meanwhile, of course, the proportion of manual workers applying for places at the Open University remains very low. As with the university scholarship (grants) provisions of the 1944 Education Act, it is the white collar (or black-coated) sector of the labor force which has taken advantage of a new equalization of educational opportunity. The category 'other' in the Open University's statistics and the ambiguity of the term 'technical personnel' makes comparison with other studies difficult. I do have the impression that the percentage of workers applying to the Open University is no higher and may well be lower than the percentage of workers' children at other universities. The familiar psychic and material barriers are at work: fewer sources of information, an inability to see the uses of culture, the conviction that these are matters for 'them' and not for 'us', the sheer fatigue and economic constraints of manual work. These are not difficulties which can be overcome by a widespread advertising campaign. An educated working class, a class in full possession of a national tradition (why should not railwaymen and engineers know Shakespeare and Lawrence, and appreciate the theorems of physics?) awaits a much fuller development of projects like the Open University.

However, society is organized in a way which makes very strong the forces denying the working class access to a high culture. I have indirectly intimated that a considerable amount of the spiritual investment in the Open University may be thought of as a secularized version of socialism (a statistical study of the political composition of its teachers, administrators and students would be rewarding). My term may not be just. The belief in the mission of the Open University, for some, may be a form of socialism transposed or spiritualized. If so, they had best think again. The provision of educational opportunity may be thought of as an important component of any socialist programme worthy of the name: it will not alter the relations of property and power.

Indeed, there is an aspect of the Open University which must (and does) appeal to prescient technocrats unburdened by socialist aspirations. The project seems to represent an answer, if by no means the only one, to the problem of rising educational costs. The Conservative Government's insistence on the admission of eighteen-year-old school-leavers makes sense in this context. Witness the rush to import large features of the Open University to the United States. Not since our millionaires purchased entire Scottish castles and had them shipped here stone by stone has there been such crass cultural transfer. The socialist tradition which ennobled Messrs Wilson and Short and Miss Jennie Lee hardly has an American counterpart. It is the economy promised by the Open University that is so attractive in this country (as well as a totally unfounded belief that the Open University can be assimilated to some current efforts to reduce the pain of higher education by random experimentation with new university forms).

No doubt, the Open University is an experiment which can test the social need for continuing education. The provision of opportunity for a second chance at higher education for those adults who missed theirs the first time around is important, but here too we should be aware of the technocratic imperatives at work: the availability of social investment for this purpose is connected with the changing composition of the labour force, the increase in its educational attainments made necessary by technological development. In this connection, I note with a certain scepticism the provision for close consultation between the Open University and the various professional, technical, and economic bodies concerned with the educational recycling of the labor force. Education for citizenship may consist, primarily, of what is at the moment highly impractical. I do not justify my scepticism on the basis of the putative superiority of cultural over technical education. It is the capacity to understand the social uses of technique that alone can enable contemporary populations to withstand a (possibly comfortable) servitude to technocratic rulers.

Is the Open University a step in the direction of society organized as a colossal university, a permanent learning system? Here, we cross the threshold of fantasy. The image of society as educational system has its heuristic uses, but it allows no boundaries between reflection and action. Stated in overly simple terms, it can encourage the narcissism of the academy. The essential questions concern the aims and contents of higher education. Much of our university culture has been ossified, even mandarinized. An educated citizenry cannot be composed of doctors of philosophy, particularly in an epoch in which academic specialization has emptied that degree of any value associated with an older understanding of philosophy as *sagesse*. It is at this point that the Open University may make an interesting contribution to the general problem of higher education.

The Open University's teachers, to judge by the evidence in these pages, are thinking hard about the ends of higher education. The necessity of devising new instructional techniques and programs for teaching at a distance, the problem of distinguishing essential from inessential matter in our inherited curricular structures, has obviously stimulated reflection. Of course, curricular discussion (in committee), and reflection on the ends of education (in books by academic dignitaries who have long since quit the infertile terrain of their classrooms for the greener pastures of educational management) are conspicuous features of the current literature on universities. Rarely, however, have they been brought into such close contact with the daily teaching enterprise.

The process of reflection seems most advanced in the fields of technology and science. The Open University's technologists think that it is indispensable to teach the general nature of technological process, a relationship of mastery over nature mediated by the instrumentality of a system. The scientists suppose that what is fundamental is, in effect, a concept of evidence and an attitude toward it. In the world's oldest industrial nation, it is indeed time that the descendants of Newton, Watt and Darwin cease to repeat that only Greek and Latin can train the mind. Scientific and technological education at the Open University, clearly, consists of something other than a smattering of knowledge about the pure and applied sciences. It is an effort to apprehend a legacy in new terms, and it is rather consciously directed to obverting a technocratic capture of knowledge. The situation in the humanities and social sciences, to judge by the course materials I have seen, is somewhat less clear cut. There I sense no such explicit avowal of a new pedagogic purpose. In all fairness, traces of the search for one are certainly visible. In all the areas of learning, the very limitations under which the Open University functions provide a clearer experimental field than in conventional universities.

The absense of a geographically localized learning community, the absence of close (and sometimes daily) contact with other students and with teachers, poses the problem of the transmission of high culture in an acute form. In his remarkable essay, 'The Work of Art in the Age of its Mechanical Reproduction,' Walter Benjamin described the loss of the aura of uniqueness of the art work in our age. Mechanically reproduced art completed the emancipation of art from ritual. Art for art's sake was an earlier ideological response to the desacralization of art, but that too has proven an untenable position. Analogically, we may say that the transmission of high culture has gradually freed itself of ecclesiastical and religious domination. The doctrine of liberal learning for its own sake, was (like the idea of art for art's sake) a phase in the secularization of the university—even if uttered by a Cardinal. The aura that has now been lost is the aura attached to high culture as an expression of a bourgeois (or in terms of our English-speaking cultures) middle class society. The distance across which the Open University transmits culture is not alone geographical; it is social.

The communal structure of universities has been an indispensable condition of education—understood as the induction of students into modes of thought and perception. Culture, in these circumstances, was, among other things, also specific to an entire range of class-related attitudes and behavior. It is true that radio and television will bring teachers, episodically, into students' homes. It is also true that they remain in their homes, workplaces, and milieux. Not all of these, to be sure, are impossibly remote from the cultural concerns of the university. Distance remains.

I have cast about for a term to describe the process represented by the Open University's technical utilization of the means of mass culture for the transmission of high culture. A completion of the desacralization of learning, surely, but also a form of purification of it: an attempt, no matter how inexplicit and tentative, to free it of class-bound elements. Perhaps the attempt can be made on such a scale only in a society like Britain, where the middle class has been so dominant culturally that its universities have rarely questioned their own class character. A contradiction with what I said earlier about the Open University's socialist antecedents? I do not think so: British socialism always rested on ideas of the accession to culture by the nation. The Open University's students, in their willingness to accept academic subject matter, attest their belief in the universality of that subject matter—in what we may understand as its higher utility. The project is quite different from an American tradition expressed by Cornell's 'any person, any study' or by contemporary continental ventures like the German *Gesamthochschule*, with its fluidity of boundaries between sectors of education. Perhaps the discussions with the polytechnics, reported as I write, mark a certain attenuation of the Open University's initial assumptions. I hope not, and I find it encouraging that these discussions occur simultaneously with discussions with universities like Lancaster. If the Open University, however, is to become the first post-bourgeois university—a number of tasks remain before it. Not the least of these is the beginning of a serious process of conceptual self-reflection, as distinct from the (entirely laudable) programme of research it has begun. Indeed, the two processes will have to conjoin from time to time.

In the meantime, in the absence of a localized learning community, it is striking that relatively few students have sought to organize study groups on their own. No doubt, the obstacles in their way—not least, absence of time—have been considerable. Individualized notions of the personal appropriation of a fixed and objective subject matter must also play their part: the Open University's students are traditional in their beliefs about their relationships to culture. Their interesting, not infrequently moving, accounts of their struggles and joys with their studies invariably express a single spirit's encounter with the world. Surely, at some point the Open University itself must confront its students with the demand that they reflect on their mode of study. I do not for one moment propose a vertiginous descent into the absured subjectivism which has marked the retreat from culture in some experimenting American circles. I think it likely that there may be increased emphasis in the future of the Open University on local study groups, on tutorial resources, weekend and summer schools—not to mention the possibilities of exchanges, by the students, with other institutions of higher education. In that case, it is legitimate to expect that the alteration in the form of study should occasion serious discussion between teachers and students.

One thing about the Open University, if I may continue to employ the term, is already post-bourgeois: its mode of intellectual production. Much is made, in the text, of the difficulties with the demands of teamwork for university teachers raised in a virtuoso tradition. That tradition is, actually, inauthentic: most academic individualists reproduce, with marginal idiosyncrasies, the prevailing assumptions and styles of the university milieux in which they developed. It is striking that our universities, populated by characterological individualists, are so unpluralistic intellectually. It is necessary to distinguish between the psychological and the cultural components of the discussion. No doubt, there is an aesthetic satisfaction for the producer in making a total (and visibly total) intellectual product. However, most intellectual products quickly enough are integrated into other totalities: currents of discussion and debate, short-range traditions. Indeed, where intellectual work is much more cumulative, in the natural sciences, teamwork is quite customary. There is ample evidence that intellectual and aesthetic products generated in and by groups are not inferior to individually produced ones: what about Gothic cathedrals, or contemporary films, quite apart from Nobel-Prize winning pieces of research in the sciences?

The group or team mode of organization has nothing intrinsically superior about it. Anyone who has suffered through meetings of academic committees, departments, faculties, will be tempted to effect a very slight modification in that citation from *The Pickwick Papers* about the law being an ass. However, nothing is eternally right about our present academic division of labor. The conflicts entailed in course production for the Open University may constitute necessary steps on the way to curricular rethinking. The Open University's organizational experiment may form a new generation of academics, able to use a far wider range of concepts and methods, capable of relating knowledge to the aims of inquiry rather than to the rigidities of fixed disciplines. Most interdisciplinary ventures (the various General Education programs in the United States, the ill-fated *Stadium Generale* in the immediate post-war German universities, the Schools at Sussex, the *pluridisciplinarité* of Vincennes) have after a time become centrifugal: the claims of the disciplines reassert themselves. This tendency is, clearly, not absent at the Open University: it ought to be resisted.

Perhaps the Open University can move from its initial foundation courses, through rather more specific ones, to advanced integrative courses for the first degree. Its post-graduate instruction ought not to mimic the fragmentation and tenuousness of the organization of knowledge in the separate disciplines. Its post-experience courses could be directed to devising a new notion of the relationship between knowledge and practise. These are, of course, easy demands to raise an ocean away; the fact that I raise them expresses a fascination with the Open University which is far from private.

The Open University's potential contribution to higher education, then, may not reside exclusively in its economic and technological dimensions. So far from the OU having to borrow from existing institutions, in the best case we may look forward to a situation in which the ou helps the rest of us reconsider our curricular assumptions. The Open University has begun with a fairly straightforward notion of subject matter, which assumes that students have much to learn from an intact cultural tradition. Its problems in communicating that tradition, however, are not merely technical. Like all university teachers, our colleagues at the Open University have to ask: what remains, what can be taught? What I have termed its post-bourgeois form may well facilitate the search for an answer—providing that the common academic fallacy of confusing form and content is surmounted.

Part III

The students and the system

Chapter 5

Admissions policy

Ray Thomas
Senior Lecturer in Economics and Acting Director, New Towns Study Group

My interest in admissions policy derives partly from studies which I have made of Britain's New Towns at Political and Economic Planning in London. Seeing both the Open University and the New Towns as promoting upward social mobility, in this article I consider the question: 'Upward social mobility for whom?'

'What is the Open University for?' Should it, at one extreme, be a kind of liberal arts college giving degrees in traditional academic subjects like mathematics, theoretical physics, sociology, music and philosophy? Or should it, at the other extreme, be a kind of polytechnic attempting to teach semi-vocational skills in the hope that it will identify the kinds of skills which will enable its students materially to better themselves in an age of rapidly changing technology?

These questions inevitably hinge upon admissions policy because the kind of student admitted inevitably influences the nature of the courses offered. So who applies for places and who gets admitted?

It is university policy that no formal academic qualifications are necessary for registration as a student. Formal qualifications are not even taken into account in the selection process, and partly as a result of this policy little information is available on the educational characteristics of applicants. Of the first 30,000 applicants for 1971 places, 5 per cent already held a degree. For 37 per cent a teacher's certificate was the highest educational qualification. Sixteen per cent possessed a professional qualification, and 11 per cent a GCE 'A' level or Higher School Certificate. Thus less than one-third of applicants would be regarded as unqualified entrants by the standards of most British universities.

Indications of educational qualification are provided by the occupation of applicants shown in Table 1. More than one-third

47

of applicants for places in 1971 came from teachers. It appears that less than one in every ten applications are from manual workers. (Though this statement can be true only if housewives are counted as non-manual workers.)

Table 1   Applications by occupation (percentages)

	For study in year			
	1971	*1972*	*1973*	*1974*
Housewives	9·2	11·0	13·0	14·6
Administrators and managers	6·9	4·6	4·3	3·6
Teachers and lecturers	35·9	30·2	29·6	28·3
The professions and the arts	11·9	12·6	11·6	11·6
Qualified scientists and engineers	8·0	4·4	3·7	3·0
Technical personnel	7·5	11·9	11·2	9·8
Clerical and office staff	8·2	9·4	9·7	10·5
Shopkeepers and service workers	3·4	4·4	4·4	4·4
Other	8·9	11·5	12·5	14·3
Total number of applicants	43,444	35,182	32,046	35,011

The pattern of change in the occupations of applicants may be significant. The proportions of teachers, administrators and managers, and qualified scientists and engineers have all declined slightly. The proportion of housewives and technicians has increased. The increase in the proportion of applications from technicians is at least in part attributable to the introduction of a Foundation Course in technology in 1972. But the other changes suggest that the university may be becoming of interest to members of a wider variety of occupational groups.

The geographical pattern of applications seems to reflect the occupational pattern. A high proportion of applications relative to population come from the south-eastern parts of England and a low proportion relative to population from all other areas (although, exceptionally, the number from Northern Ireland is relatively high). Thus for 1972, 42·7 per cent of applications came from the London, south-east, and south regions, and east Anglia, although these four Open University regions accounted for only 34·9 per cent of the United Kingdom's adult population in 1971.

The variables considered so far all relate to the background of applicants. Some indication of what these applicants want is given by the Foundation Course preferences shown in Table 2. In the first year 62 per cent of applicants opted for arts or social science and this percentage was maintained for 1972 in spite of the introduction of a Foundation Course in technology. For 1973 the proportion opting for arts and social science increased to 65 per cent, and for 1974 to 68 per cent.

Table 2   Applications by Foundation Course

(first preferences for one-course applicants, first two preferences for two-course applicants)

	Numbers (and percentages)			
	1971	*1972*	*1973*	*1974*
Arts	16,939	12,344	11,678	13,128
	(27·3)	(29·2)	(31·6)	(33·2)
Social science	21,564	13,918	12,314	13,634
	(34·7)	(32·9)	(33·3)	(34·4)
Mathematics	12,039	6,277	5,426	5,168
	(19·4)	(14·8)	(14·7)	(13·0)
Science	11,605	5,434	4,134	4,511
	(18·7)	(12·8)	(11·2)	(11·4)
Technology	—	4,346	3,396	3,209
		(10·3)	(9·2)	(8·1)
Total course applications	62,147	42,319	36,957	39,650

The mechanics of the system

At a very early stage in the life of the university it was decided that admissions should operate on the 'first come first served' principle. Although suggestions have been made for some element of random selection these suggestions have so far been rejected mainly on the grounds that date of application is a means by which the applicant can influence his chance of being selected.

Three other factors are taken into account in the selection system—achieving course, regional and occupational quotas. The course quotas adopted are shown in Table 3.

Regional quotas have up to the present been set to redress the imbalance in applications; the percentage of places allocated to a region is fixed at half-way between the percentage of applications from that region and the percentage of total population living in that region. Occupational quotas in 1971 and 1972 were set to correspond fairly closely to the pattern of applications.

Table 3   Target admissions by Foundation Course

	1971	*1972*	*1973*	*1974*
Arts	8,000	6,200	5,000	4,200
Social science	8,000	7,200	6,000	5,040
Mathematics	7,000	4,450	3,780	2,520
Science	7,000	4,500	3,340	2,520
Technology	—	1,850	2,320	2,520
Total course places	25,000	24,200	20,440	16,800
Total student places	20,000	20,500	17,000	15,000

The selection process is conducted using a computer. The first come first served principle provides the basis for the system. But the date of some applications are, in effect, advanced or retarded in the queue according to course, region and occupation in order to obtain a new ranking of applications. In 1972 for example, applications for the foundation course in mathematics, science and technology were advanced by the equivalent of about two months relative to applications for the courses in arts and social science. Applications for places in Wales were advanced by about two months relative to applications for places in the south region.

Applications from male teachers and male technicians were retarded by about a month. Applications from housewives and female clerical workers were advanced by about a fortnight.

Public knowledge of the university

Knowledge of the university depends primarily upon the mass media. The university is given a great deal of coverage by the *Guardian,* the *Daily Telegraph, The Times, The Times Higher Education Supplement* and many other specialist publications. The press department had, by mid-1972, sent out more than 450 press releases and had already accumulated more than 8,000 press cuttings. But the university receives little coverage in the mass circulation newspapers. Eighty per cent of the readers of the *Guardian* are aware of the university, but only one-third of *Mirror* readers are aware of the university's existence. The university obtains publicity through its broadcasts on BBC and VHF radio, but it is university policy that these broadcasts are complementary to the correspondence units, and they are not intended to appeal to the public at large nor necessarily to be comprehensible to listeners or viewers who haven't studied the correspondence units or the broadcast notes. Existing students are probably an important source of knowledge, and in 1972 a letter was sent to students asking them to inform their friends of the opportunities the university offers.

The coverage the university receives and the publicity it gets through broadcasts is supplemented by a certain amount of advertising. The *Radio Times* has published several features on the university. The university has advertised in the *Daily Express*, *Daily Mail* and *Daily Mirror* specifically to attract applications from skilled manual workers. It has also advertised in regional papers to help reduce the imbalance in the pattern of applications by region.

Policy issues

Many people believe that the university should play a greater role in extending university education to members of the lower socio-economic groups. But it is difficult to see how this could be achieved. It is arguable that the university has already become more widely known in a few years, mainly through its use of the mass media, than the Workers' Educational Association has in decades. Advertising and other forms of publicity could be designed specifically to inform specific groups, but it is doubtful whether providing information would by itself have much effect in stimulating applications from members of the working classes. To make the man on the factory floor respond a hard sell may well be necessary.

Reader's Digest and book clubs make extensive use of direct mail advertising. Encyclopaedia publishers often use door-to-door salesmen. The publishers of 'part works' use TV advertising. But a hard sell to a mass market would need a far heavier expenditure than is currently allowed for in the Open University advertising budget.

A hard sell would also involve a change of role of publicity. If the aim is to change attitudes as well as inform it might, for example, be appropriate to stress the income and status advantages of possession of a degree. But to convince the factory worker that a degree might protect him against the danger of unemployment or might lead to a career rather than a job would require more pointed slogans than 'The Open University is doing fine—so come on in' which was the heading of the *Radio Times* feature in January 1972.

There would be no justification, however, for stressing the income and status advantages of a degree unless these were in fact qualities of the product. This comes back to the question posed at the beginning of the chapter. Should the university be putting on courses of a predominantly academic character or should there be vocational or semi-vocational courses? Should the Open University become in fact an Open Polytechnic?

At the foundation level the number of students is measured in thousands and the university is able to take full advantage of the division of labour and economies of scale. But a widening variety of courses is and will be offered at second and subsequent levels. Student numbers per course will be measured in hundreds rather than thousands. The economics of many courses will depend upon attracting sufficient students. It would be surprising therefore if faculties did not attempt to cut the garment to suit the cloth in second and higher level courses, which might result in a preponderance of courses for teachers and courses of a narrowly academic character.

The development of post-experience courses illustrates the nature of the dilemma. Beginning in 1973 the university admitted occasional students for post-experience courses which are designed, among other purposes, for those 'who, after practising their profession for some years, are called upon to make a significant advance or change in their occupation'.

During the winter of 1971–2 more than a million people in Britain were unemployed. Many of them had already in effect been called upon to change their occupation. During the next few decades the number of factory workers is likely to continue to decline and the number of white collar workers will continue to grow. Post-experience courses could play some part in facilitating changes from blue collar to white collar occupations. But shouldn't the undergraduate courses also fulfil a role of this kind? If so why should there be a distinction between those courses leading to a degree and the post-experience courses?

Chapter 6

The OU student

Naomi McIntosh

Head of Survey Research Department

The typical Open University student is a man, in his thirties, in a white-collar job; although he is now apparently middle-class, his parents were probably working-class and he himself may well still call himself working-class. He has clearly already been involved in a lot of study, either 'full' or 'part-time', and thus has been able to move on to a different sort of job from his parents. But he is an orthodox type, reading the *Daily Telegraph* and spending most of his remaining leisure time on TV, gardening and do-it-yourself. Seven out of ten students are men.

Obviously with a new educational institution, those who started studying with us first are those who heard about us first. Even in our second year (1972), only 40 per cent of the population as a whole had heard about the Open University and this varied greatly across different social classes, from 78 per cent among the upper and middle classes to 22 per cent among the working-class. So it was not surprising that teachers, for instance, figured high in our first year's intake.

We have had to meet in the first year or so of the university's life the backlog of demand for a 'second chance' at education which is not likely to recur. The pattern of demand for the Open University is likely to change over the next few years. What may well happen is a growth in the idea that people can and should move in and out of education as and when they need or wish to do so. This may be either to take full degree courses or to take shorter courses which fulfil a particular need at a particular time.

Although we have not yet overcome the traditional pattern of discrimination between men and women going on to higher education, our proportions are no worse than other universities and better than most polytechnics and technical colleges. On some courses, women are more equal than others; 50 per cent of humanities students in 1972 were women, compared with 12 per cent of maths and 6 per cent of technology. But it will take more than the mere existence of the ou to eradicate years of tradition in schools and elsewhere against women studying science and maths. Each year so far has seen a higher proportion of women applying, which is encouraging—particularly since, once in, they stay in rather better than the men.

Age, education and occupation

The university was set up to give a second chance to adults, and 'adult' was initially interpreted as being twenty-one and over. The largest group of students are in their late twenties and early thirties, followed by those in their late thirties and early forties. There has already been a significant shift downwards in the age distribution—twice as many in their early twenties registered in 1972 as in 1971. It is worth watching this trend since younger students in 1971 and 1972 did not stay in as well as older ones, a fact which has to be taken into account as there is increased pressure on the university to play its part in the expansion of higher education by accepting eighteen-year-olds.

Table 1   Date of birth of students provisionally registered (percentages)

	1971	*1972*
Date of birth		
1946 and later	10	21
1936–1945	39	40
1926–1935	31	24
1916–1925	16	12
1915 or earlier	4	3

Table 2 shows the occupational categories of students in our first two years. Teachers, in particular, dominated our first year. Perhaps we should count the benefit to our children and our educational system in having educated, up-dated and refreshed teachers. But I myself was glad to see a wider variety of occupa-

Table 2   Occupation of students provisionally registered in January 1971 and 1972 (percentages)

	1971	*1972*
Housewives	9·3	12·5
Armed forces	1·7	2·0
Admin. and managers	5·2	5·1
Education	37·0	30·1
Professions and arts	8·9	12·0
Scientists and engineers	6·5	4·5
Technical personnel	12·4	13·0
Skilled trades and other manual	3·9	5·9
Clerical and office staff	6·7	8·5
Shop, personal service	3·5	4·1
Retired, in institutions, no information	5·1	3·0

tional backgrounds joining the OU in 1972. They bring with them not just a lower average age, but fewer formal educational qualifications. In 1972 the groups without the 'formal' entry qualifications for conventional universities rose from one-quarter (in 1971) to one-third of the students (Table 3). It will be on the success or failure of these 'formally' less well qualified students that our claim to be an Open University will stand or fall.

This lack of formal educational qualification is borne out by the analysis of the age at which our students had completed their 'normal' full-time education. Four-fifths, in 1971, had experience of part-time education. In 1972 this had dropped to two in every three—still a high proportion, but another pointer to a changing population, less well equipped to cope with study difficulties (see Figure 1). About one in three had left school at sixteen or under, another third between seventeen and twenty, and the remaining third had continued until twenty-one and over. These differing educational backgrounds point up the difficulties for academics in deciding at what level to pitch the foundation courses. To start too high will inevitably leave some behind, and belie the openness of the first year. To start too low may underestimate others' abilities and bore them into leaving.

All of this presents an oversimplified view of what our students are like and from what backgrounds they come. We have been able to find out much more about them from a longitudinal study (funded initially by the ssRc) which has looked at their educational, occupational and family backgrounds, their home environment, and study conditions, their leisure and other

*Table 3 Highest educational level attained
by students provisionally registered in
January 1971 and 1972 (percentages)*

	1971	*1972*
No formal qualifications	6·8	8·6
CSE or RAS	1·8	3·8
GCE 'O' level 1–4 subjects	5·9	7·6
GCE 'O' level 5 or more	10.8	12·8
GCE 'A' level 1 subject	3·6	4·1
GCE 'A' level 2 or more	9·5	9·2
ONC/OND	3·8	5·1
HNC/HND	10·7	10·6
Teachers certificate	28·9	24·0
University diploma	8·6	7·4
University degree	4·1	5·3
No information	5·6	1·5

interests. This study is designed to follow students throughout their university career. Although we do not yet know enough about which particular students have continued with us, we do know that some groups stayed on to final registration in our first year at a higher rate than others. There was little difference between the regions, with the exception of London and Scotland which both lost rather more students. No other region registered changes either way of more than 1 per cent.

The highest proportion to withdraw came from the skilled manual workers. This is a group under some stress, with demanding jobs, but not necessarily supportive employers or much time off. More of these students were studying maths and science, faculties with a higher withdrawal rate and heavy work-loads.

Figure 1   *Terminal age of full-time education—1972 students*

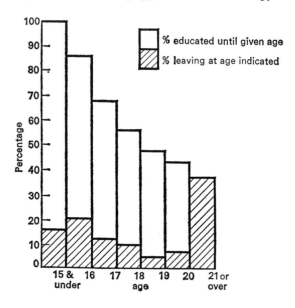

Housewives' persistence was seen most in the arts faculty, although they stayed in rather better across all faculties. The administrative/management group stayed in better only in social science, not unexpectedly. Teachers stayed in best across all the faculties, but particularly in maths.

Significantly more women than men continued to final registration. These show up almost entirely in the humanities Foundation Course (the housewives). There was also a trend towards older students staying in at a higher rate. The youngest age-group, born post-1945, had fallen out significantly more, and the largest age-group, born 1936–45 had also withdrawn at a slightly higher rate.

Not surprisingly the groups with no formal qualifications, or less than five 'O' levels, were most vulnerable. This was particularly marked in science and maths. In maths you had to have two 'A' levels or an HNC/HND or above to stay in 'better'. In science the change point was lower—at one 'A' level. The ONC/OND group here also held its own.

Figure 2 *Student progress by course.* 100% = *all students finally registered for each Foundation Course, 1971*

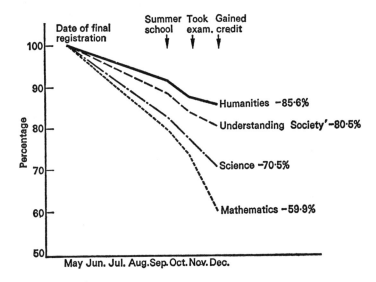

Social class

The problem of measuring, let alone defining 'social class' is one that sociologists and others have argued about for years. There is little or no agreement on any objective measure of social class, and many varying classifications, both objective and subjective are currently in use. Table 4 shows a cross-analysis of what class the students subjectively consider they belong to and what one standard semi-objective classification, used for most media and market research surveys (the IPA classification), would have put them in.

Taking the market research classification (based on present job and income) shows only 8 per cent as working class, as compared with 15 per cent who rated *themselves* as 'working-class'. But if one were to take the standard way in which students in higher education are normally categorized, that is by the occupation of their father at the time the student entered higher education, then on these criteria, about two-thirds of our students would be classified

Table 4   Social class of students: objective and self-rated

	Total	Upper middle (A)	Middle (B)	Lower middle (C1)	Skilled working (C2)	Working (D)	Lowest level (E)
Base—all students in sample = 100%	4,199	139 (3%)	2,079 (50%)	1,545 (37%)	301 (7%)	45 (1%)	8
Social self-rating (%)							no.
Upper	1	1	0	1	0	0	(0)
Upper middle	6	35	6	4	2	—	(0)
Middle	38	49	44	34	18	20	(0)
Lower middle	26	6	26	29	25	18	(1)
Working	15	3	10	18	37	40	(4)
Don't know	7	3	6	8	7	11	(2)
Other answers	7	5	7	6	11	11	(1)

* Breakdown excludes those 2% for whom we had inadequate information.

as working-class. Table 5 compares male students' occupations with fathers' jobs during the students' later years of schooling. It is reasonable to consider, at minimum, groups 7, 8 and 9 as predominantly working-class.

Table 5   O U male students' occupations compared with fathers' occupations

Open University occupational categories	Fathers' jobs during students' later years of schooling	Present job of male students
1 Armed forces	3	2
2 Admin. and managers	5	8
3 Education	3	40
4 Professions and arts	6	8
5 Qualified scientists	3	9
6 Technical personnel	1	10
7 Skilled manual and other manual workers	45	8
8 Clerical and office staff	7	6
9 Shop, personal services	15	5
10 Retired, not working, not known	13	3

Universities have traditionally been avenues of upward social mobility, although the Robbins report showed a decade ago that the proportion of working-class children going to University had not effectively been increased with the expansion of higher education. Recent studies of polytechnic students indicate they may well be no more working-class than those from universities (Donaldson, 1971). What is different about the Open University is that, as adults, our students have already moved away from their parental origins. But taken at that time, they would have been more working-class than students in any other British university. Taken now, they have already moved, many of them, into white-collar jobs and professions. Nevertheless their working-class origins are clear. An alternative analysis by socio-economic class paints the same picture (Table 6).

Table 6   OU Students' social class compared with their fathers' social class

		Father's social grade (IPA)						
	Total	Upper middle	Middle	Lower middle	Skilled working	Working	Lowest level	No answer
Base—all students in sample = 100%	4,199	114 (3%)	696 (17%)	785 (19%)	1,561 (37%)	522 (12%)	3	518 (12%)
Student's social grade (%)							no.	
Upper middle class	3	17	6	3	2	1	(0)	3
Middle class	50	46	55	45	51	50	(0)	45
Lower middle class	37	32	34	43	35	37	(2)	39
Skilled working class	7	2	3	7	9	9	(0)	6
Working class	1	2	1	1	1	1	(1)	1
Lowest subsistence level	0	0	0	0	0	0	(0)	0
No answer/ unclassifiable	2	1	1	1	2	1	(0)	6

This is an important point to remember when tendentious comparisons are made, but the point is still only of limited value. It only tells us about one aspect of educational disadvantage, and more importantly, only tells us about the past and not about the future.

In response to a specific question, about 30 per cent of the students answered that they would have liked to stay on longer at school than they were able to. The reasons which prevented them were predominantly financial. This was often tied up with the death of a parent, coming from a large family, unemployment, etc. A significant group, particularly girls, left early because of parental resistance.

Students and their studies

We have built up an elaborate system of radio and television programmes, written materials, study centres for individual personal support and so on. But we had to decide to do this on faith, and had no way of knowing whether it would work or whether this was what students really needed. A panel of students are reporting to us regularly week by week on how they are using the system, and we have already changed parts of it which clearly created problems.

Major research questions which have occupied us have inevitably been those that touch on areas either where the university has had to decide to spend a lot of money, or where the constraints of how students live and work are likely materially to affect their ability to utilize and obtain maximum advantage from the educational materials provided. The first two years have shown encouraging high levels of viewing and listening. Sizable proportions of students have gone out of their way to watch the programmes twice, particularly in science and maths.

Table 7 compares the viewing figures over two faculties for 1971 and 1972 over a sample of weeks in the middle of the academic year. The majority of students as was originally planned have chosen to watch or listen at home, around 70–80 per cent across all faculties. Increasingly larger numbers are taping programmes at home so they can listen to them at their leisure. One note of warning for the future is the seeming reluctance of students to take advantage of the re-play facilities which are also available at study centres.

Table 7   Percentage of students viewing TV programmes

TV programme No.	6	7	8	9	10	11
Arts						
1971	92	90	no prog.	90	90	93
1972	91	83	84	89	89	91
Science						
1971	99	96	98	97	97	97
1972	95	92	91	95	95	95

The use of study centres is a matter of some interest and constant argument. How much of our resources are we justified in putting into providing a pale replica of traditional face-to-face tuition? Would we not do better to concentrate on developing better support for independent learning? The use which students make of study centres varies over the times of the year. In the early weeks many students attend—mainly to see counsellors and for the students to familiarize themselves with the system (50–60 per cent of students in any oné week). Later on this drops to 30 per cent or so, reducing even more over the summer, but increasing again a little, to 40 per cent or so, as examinations approach. Some students are unable to get to study centres and 10 per cent simply prefer not to. For some, the study centres clearly provide a social experience rather than an educational experience and in times of continuing limited resources, this may need justifying.

We aimed initially at a notional work-load of about ten hours a week per full credit course. Even with developmental testing this could not always be accurately gauged. The work-load on Foundation Courses in 1971 varied across faculties, and also more conspicuously between units in one course. For example, one unit in science was particularly overloaded in 1971 (with students working an average of seventeen hours on it). This was clearly unacceptable and the science Foundation Course team in 1972 allowed two weeks for studying this unit making a later unit optional. The result is that in 1972 the 'double' unit took an average of 21 hours.

Overall as a result of the feedback from all sources the science

Faculty have developed new study guides for each unit outlining learning strategies which indicate which parts of the unit are essential and which are desirable and which are optional. They were worried that students were being over-conscientious in their early studies and aimed to reduce this over anxiety by additional advice about how to study. Results in 1972 showed this strategy to have been successful, and hours spent on science units 5–10 dropped from an average of 15·3 hours to 11·9 hours.

Studying with the Open University is in itself likely to become a way of life for some students. It will take several years for many to achieve degrees. High proportions of the optimists who started studying two courses have each year dropped down from two to one (30 per cent in 1971 and 40 per cent in 1972). Obviously different types of students are opting for different courses; many teachers who studied social science or arts, as a Foundation Course are now specializing in education and constitute the vast majority of continuing education faculty students. Only in technology does any one occupational group outnumber teachers, where technical personnel number one-third of all students. Neither is age a bar to success with the OU as a small but significant number of students in their sixties and seventies prove vociferously. The heterogeneity of our students, and the new ways in which they learn pose new questions which have not conventionally been asked or answered in higher education.

Chapter 7

The OU in the south-west

Dudley Buckingham
Regional Director, south-west region

The summer schools in the first year were as good for the university as they were for the students. Students found the relief, reassurance and the stimulus which came from a new sense of belonging and the recognition that there were other students with exactly the same problems. Study difficulties encountered in comparative isolation were put into new and less daunting perspectives. The university, personified in its various categories of teaching staff, centrally and regionally based, gained valuable insights into the realities of the student situation. The summer schools still remain the best examples of unified university effort. I wonder, however, how long my regional staff can maintain their enthusiasm for meeting the impossible deadlines which the establishment of a mini-residential university for seven weeks each summer demand. The prospect not of fewer schools but of more, as each year passes, provides no crumb of comfort. In my less sane moments I begin to picture the university as a monster which sprouts new heads each year.

Whilst preparation for more and more summer schools begins to present some horrifying prospects, working at the schools themselves is a tremendously rewarding and exhilarating experience. Students' loyalty to the institution even in the first difficult year was revealed in their sharp reaction to occasional hostile criticism from some outside academics who took part-time teaching posts at the schools. It was as if they felt that only those who suffered under the system had the right to criticize it.

Of all the university's committees in which I participate I still find the most stimulating to be the south-west regional Consultative Committee when representatives of the region's students and staff, part time and full time, meet to discuss the monster we have together created. Like the summer school it permits a clearer view of what it is really like to be an independent adult learner. All university students tend to exhibit anxiety symptoms at some stage in their studies. The ou student is particularly vulnerable.

Whatever the merits of administrative decentralization, the key to the university's regional operation is to be found here. It lies in the recognition that external students need some kind of local support. The regional staff are there to assist the student in overcoming problems inherent in learning at a distance. We exist in Bristol, as we do in Manchester, to provide some reassurance and tutorial help for our diverse student population.

What may be possible, however, in Manchester or London may not be possible or even desirable for students in Bristol. What may present a solution for students in Bristol may have little relevance in Barnstaple. The regional task is to assist in the formation of central schemes of reinforcement and to interpret, adapt and modify these so that their implementation is both feasible and useful within the individual regional and sub-regional conditions which apply.

The south-west region stretches from the softness of the Cotswolds to the rugged shorelines of the Cornish coast and beyond to the Isles of Scilly. Lands End is over 200 miles from our most northerly point in Gloucestershire. The people of Devon and Cornwall find it difficult to accept that Bristol can be their regional headquarters. A region of this size, curiously elongated, has few large centres of population. Whilst the total student population is small compared with regions like London and the north-west, it is scattered both in terms of geography and subject spread. Travel is no easier in the winter months than it is in other regions. In the summer, because of the tourist invasion, it is a good deal more difficult. In these circumstances the evening tutorial and counselling sessions for all students, first, second and third level, which can be held in study centres in the London region, are often not possible at all for many students. Saturday schools three or four times a year are the most we can sometimes provide. If you are a student living at Penzance and the day school is in Plymouth you are still 67 miles away. What kind of local tutorial pattern can be provided if there are but twenty philosophy students spread throughout the 5,500 square miles which make up the south-west? If one defines as 'disadvantaged' those students who cannot receive BBC 2 or VHF signals, those students who because of distance cannot visit their nearest study centres, those who cannot attend Saturday day schools, then of our 2,600 student population, we can count four hundred as being in this category in the south-west. These students suffer from a sense of isolation even within their normal living patterns. They often live in areas where job and education opportunities are limited. Many indeed see the Open University as a route to escape from economic deprivation. These students largely survive because of their own resilience and tenacity. To assist them our part-time counsellors spend much more time than their formal contracts require. Sometimes it is possible to provide an extra injection of academic help to get the students over the particular obstacles which hold them back.

One of the regional tasks is to create (not simply recruit) a corps of skilled correspondence teachers. Teaching practices in conventional universities, with some exceptions, tend to be generally deficient; but resident students have other ways of compensating. As the OU develops its higher level courses, it must call upon the services of more subject specialists in other universities to act as its correspondence tutors. The regions will need to train such specialists in the art of teaching and more particularly in the skills of teaching at a distance. This is particularly true of regions like the south-west where the opportunities for face-to-face correctives are so restricted.

Even if we are able to devise suitable training programmes, the limited supply of subject specialists will cause difficulties. Ideally we would like tutors who live within reasonable distances of their students. Clearly this is impossible in a region like ours. The additional requirements whereby day schools in some science-based courses need to be fully equipped laboratories make for yet further complications. What began as a neat national scheme of local counselling and tutorial support based on strategically placed study centres, within three years, has turned into a major planning exercise, with new solutions having to be found each academic year.

Fortunately in the south-west the OU venture was generally greeted with enthusiasm by the Local Education Authorities, the adult education bodies and educational institutions. Bristol Polytechnic and Exeter University assisted with secondment of experienced members of their staff to serve in the initial building of our support network. The WEA provided us with our first office.

Without this kind of local goodwill much of what has been achieved would not have been possible.

The full-time staff in the region has grown from a modest establishment of five to thirty-two within the space of three years. A brief statistical summary will help to illustrate the pace of this development:

	1971	*1972*	*1973*
Students	1,151	2,245	2,651
Study centres	14	16	16
Saturday schools	—	291	489
Summer schools	7 weeks (2,500 students)	7 weeks (2,500 students)	7 weeks (4,000 students)

During this time we have had to mount many rescue operations, undoubtedly the most heroic being during the postal strike of 1971.

At the centre, student progress must inevitably be seen as a number of symbols on a computer printout. We feel we are perpetually in the firing line attempting to remedy errors of machines which daily pump out teaching material, advice and directions from Walton Hall. It is a curious institution which we serve. Whilst it has all of the features of a massive industrial organization which puts a premium upon work schedules and deadlines it can apply none of the sanctions which late delivery call into play in the business world. When material is not out on time there are justified student complaints and it is in the study centres and at the Regional Office where we have to make the apologies and explanations. From the student's point of view there is something reassuring about the knowledge that there are known individuals at whom the brickbats can be thrown. I find no joy in the fact that my colleagues are under fire in this way. This is the most frustrating part of the regional task—to understand the reasons for delays and mistakes, but often to be powerless to correct them.

In some area of our work settled patterns have developed, but these are surprisingly few. The success or failure of the regional organization will depend on whether or not it can remain flexible enough to meet new needs as they appear.

Chapter 8

Evaluation for the OU

David Hawkridge

Director, Institute of Educational Technology

One of the comments frequently made at the Open University by visiting Americans is: 'Why did you give yourselves so little time to get started?' Even in California, they say, nothing quite like the Open University has happened. 'Why didn't you start slow and small, with a pilot project?' The Open University could have spent vast sums of money on simulations and pilot projects, on experiments and trials of a limited kind. Instead, the whole project became one vast experiment. Considerable planning risks had to be taken, in the hope that the new project would be generally and quickly successful. At the same time, the university found itself obliged to take deliberate steps to evaluate and improve on its first prototype courses and systems.

This pattern of development is by no means new in the field of technology, even if it has been rare in education until recently. Countless machines have been designed quickly as prototypes and the prototypes have been set to work in conditions which allow proper measurement of their efficiency. To ensure that its prototypes were tested and improved, the university set up the Institute of Educational Technology and provided it with manpower and funds to carry out some of the evaluation. Other groups in the university are also deeply concerned with improving the prototypes, of course, but within the Institute are staff who have training and experience in evaluating educational systems and their components.

There were many, many aspects of the Open University that needed to be evaluated, and some sort of priority list had to be drawn up. One way of ordering priorities would have been for us to put first the most expensive components of the system, on the ground that what costs most should be improved first. Another way would have been to say that problem areas come first, and particularly problem areas defined by students, who are the chief consumers in the system.

In fact we did not adopt outright either of these ways of ordering priorities. Instead, we helped to persuade the university to install 'dials and gauges' wherever it seemed vital to find out what was happening in the university's very complex network. Judgments about the points where these measuring devices should be placed were made not only by the Institute but also by many of the university's committees, on which the Institute had representatives.

The detailed list of studies going on in the Institute is too long to quote here, but it breaks down into five main areas. First, there are what we call the student based studies. These are concerned mainly with student progress and the impact of the university upon the lives of its students. They are also concerned with how the students in a particular course, as a group, are studying the course—Naomi McIntosh writes about this work (pp. 54–65). Second, we began evaluative studies of the broadcast media in 1972. These are aimed not only at analysing what the university has done so far with the broadcast media but also at deciding what new experimental programmes should be made and tested. Tony Bates describes some of this work (pp. 170–7). The other three areas are tuition and counselling research, the evaluation of written course material and studies being made of the assessment system.

The tuition and counselling research project

The rapid build-up of the university included the recruitment of a large corps of part-time staff to work in the university's study centres all over the country. Nobody knew the exact roles to be played by these staff, or the kinds of problems that students would bring to them. Against this background, we conducted some studies of what actually happened.

We carried out a sample survey early in 1971 to discover more about the people who had been recruited and how the system was operating. Recruitment was carried out at regional office level, but the survey was of course a national one. We found that the system was operating much as planned, except that counsellors were generally engaging in subject-matter instruction (at the request of students). We also found that tutors usually had less experience of adult or higher education and were more recently qualified than counsellors, but the counsellors were less likely to be working full-time in universities. Recruitment had been mainly through the printed word, rather than by word of mouth.

In the second phase of the project we were helped by the University's regionally-based full-time staff tutors and senior counsellors. They visited study centres and prepared reports of what they observed there. From these case studies we compiled a 'dossier' for use in training sessions, and drew up a list of successful counselling practices. We also monitored the type and amount of information flowing through various parts of the tutors' and counsellors' sections of the university's feedback system. We found that some of the forms provided were scarcely being used at all, others were used only in some regions and still others were just about right. The bad forms were changed or scrapped, the good ones perhaps improved slightly.

We also sent observers to about half the university's 1971 summer schools. The observers had to report the extent to which they thought stated objectives were being met, and make suggestions for improving the schools. They found that not enough time was being set aside for helping individuals and diagnosing their difficulties. Some changes were made in the 1972 schools subsequently.

In 1972 we added on new work concerned with students not using the local tuition and counselling services, the use of playback and viewing centres in the study centres, and the problems of employing the audio-tape cassettes. Naturally, there have been some other major questions that the university would like to have answered. For example, how much is *enough* tuition for third level courses? Do students who cannot receive BBC 2 have real difficulty in studying OU courses? Each year we shall start new studies. In 1972 about £10,000 was spent in this area (compared with the £1·4 millions cost of the tuition and counselling system).

The evaluation of written course material

In 1971 and 1972 we mounted several studies aimed at discovering how effectively the written course material taught and the ways in which it needed changing. These studies were of two kinds: first, we studied the attitudes of students and others towards different portions of the material and, second, we did some analyses of student performance.

We evaluated the attitudes of students towards the printed materials through a multi-purpose unit-by-unit reporting system developed by Naomi McIntosh. The results showed that most students found many of the units very interesting and not too difficult. But which were the units which had shown up as uninteresting and rather difficult? Were they always *both* uninteresting *and* difficult? Or were some difficult ones found to be very interesting? The results also showed that some courses, and a good many units within courses, were taking students much more time than the university had expected. In some cases the actual units seemed to be at fault; in others the ancillary reading seemed to be too much. In these instances, we were able to tell the course teams what had happened and advise them to some extent on what to do about it.

The attitudes of tutors and counsellors towards the written materials were collated only on an informal basis. In each Faculty, members of staff collated comments received through the university network. Inevitably, the network filtered through far more information on some units than others. The network worked best where major errors had crept into the material. On these occasions the university was able to react swiftly and send out either a printed Stop Press announcement or a broadcast message.

We analysed student performance as well, in the hope that we would find clues that would be helpful in revising course materials. Our lack of success so far is related chiefly to the nature of the assessment system and to the fact that student performance is influenced by several factors.

Studies of the assessment system

In preparation for the first year of teaching quite complex decisions had to be taken on how to design, for example, the computer-marked assignments. Most of the objective (multiple-choice) tests in use in higher education test students' power of recall rather than their ability to synthesize or to solve problems. We devoted considerable effort to the development of computer-marked tests that would demand synthesis and problem-solving.

In the long-term we want to build up a question-bank in which will be stored a wide range of questions of known characteristics. From the banked questions we can then easily construct new tests.

But more important were our studies of assessment policy. We were concerned not so much with the mechanics of operating a system as with the psychometric philosophy to be employed. At the time this chapter was written we were still at the stage of asking questions rather than having found the answers. For example, how should honours degrees be graded? If we assume that a student takes six courses, should the marks he receives be averaged, should some of the courses be weighted more heavily than others, or should only some of the courses count towards an honours degree? Will first-class honours degrees be given more often to students who select the easiest courses? How do we know which course is easiest? Is it the one in which a high percentage of students get distinctions (e.g. mathematics), or one in which a low percentage fail (e.g. humanities)?

Fundamental to these studies is the assumption in the university that the examinations represent an absolute standard, in which case appreciably more students may pass one year than the previous one, since the university has no evidence that its student population does not vary in ability. The fixing of an absolute standard in higher education is a difficult process: in fact, techniques have not yet been developed to carry it out. An absolute standard implies specification of the amount and type of knowledge or skills students must display and the depth of their understanding. Measuring this amount and depth properly is beyond the reach of existing test design, and we have much interesting work before us.

Alongside these major studies of assessment policy we carried out pilot studies and minor analyses. For example, we drew comparisons between grades awarded in different Faculties. We found that broadly speaking the arts and social science Faculty assignments tended to yield grades more tightly clustered round the mean than in science or mathematics. This pattern has been observed before in other universities, and was confirmed in the OU 1971 final examination results. Once the pattern was identified, we speculated about its causes. Were the students different? Was the subject-matter likely to yield this pattern? Did the instructions to tutors, or the monitoring system, reinforce the trend? Did the pattern bear any relationship to dropout rates in the courses? We do not have answers to all these questions yet. Some academics would claim that the differences should remain anyway. Our view is that if they are to remain we should at least have a good idea how they arose, and the university should make a conscious decision to tolerate the differences and their causes.

Another minor study we completed recently was to find out whether there was any significant relationship between the dates on which students post their assignments and the grades awarded. We studied 100 cases for each of two assignments drawn from the five 1972 Foundation Courses, 1,000 cases in all, but we found no statistically significant relationship. The assignments usually came in with a rush around the due date, and the only trend at all detectable was that the early ones tended to receive very slightly better grades. We also looked at the dates by which assignments had been posted back by the tutors and the grades they awarded, but again there was no statistically significant relationship. We did notice, however, that the return of scripts seemed to be much more spread out for some assignments than others. We are now trying to find out the reasons for this.

While we were extracting the dates and grades from the assignment forms, we also noted the kinds of comments tutors make. We know from our 1971 survey that only a small percentage of the tutors had experience of correspondence tutoring, but each of the Faculties had offered some advice on how to tutor. The tutors write on the scripts as well as on the forms, but what were they saying on the forms? Our content analysis yielded nearly 100 categories, ranging from the 'Could do better' kind of remarks to constructive comment on the subject matter.

These are examples of the kinds of evaluative studies we have undertaken so far. What of the future? There seem to be many more areas that should be studied. For example, practical work in science summer schools will be the subject of one new project. In 1974, the university's experiment in offering its courses to eighteen-year-olds will be evaluated by the Institute. We are also monitoring the experiments in using OU materials in North America although the detailed evaluation there is being carried out by Educational Testing Service at Princeton, New Jersey. In the university's regional offices there are several new projects being planned with Institute help, such as a study of remote learners in Scotland and detailed sociological observations of a study centre in the north-west.

The university offers great opportunities for many kinds of research, but there is a real concern that its students should not be turned into guinea-pigs for the sake of Brown's thesis or Robinson's paper in a journal. We are engaged in evaluative research for the university, not for research's sake but to bring about improvements wherever we can. Few other institutions of higher education have their own built-in research groups, and we are proud of these opportunities given to us.

Chapter 9

Accounting for themselves

Jennifer Rogers
BBC Further Education Officer, South

It has often been pointed out that the whole content of the typical school curriculum could be taught to adults in about one-quarter of the time and trouble it takes children. Nonetheless, the idea persists that adults make poor learners, and it is true that they face difficulties which do not apply so acutely to children.

For instance, the decay in adults of the important short-term memory facility means that information given in a lecture or demonstration cannot be efficiently learnt, especially under time pressure. Adults are anxious about looking foolish and are easily upset by academic failure. They tend to seek traditional and familiar forms of teaching and learning where, as one of the accounts in this book puts it, 'the teacher is in front'. Adult life, unlike childhood, often seems designed to make interest in learning look like an indulgence: adults have marriages, children and jobs which must be sustained first, and fatigue is always likely to come between an adult student and his books. Loss of both the learning habit and the confident familiarity with learning routines that goes with it may similarly make it hard at first to beat a steady path into formidable academic assignments.

All these difficulties predictably appear to some extent in the vivid and honest accounts in this book from o u students. Much less predictable is the astonishing sturdiness both of their own behaviour and of the new untried university system in responding to them.

Clearly, for many students the first shock was what seemed the 'harsh' comments of their tutors, no doubt many of them young graduates half their age, unused to the tenderness and cautiously phrased criticism with which adult students must be treated. Many of these essays record the bruised shock or defensive indignation with which low marks or too-tartly phrased comments were received. Adult students are hardly ever complacent; most

77

are only too easily cast down by criticism. Behind their accounts of their treatment here, one may detect perhaps some of the signs of the university itself quickly learning to adjust from the rougher frankness with which younger students may be treated in a conventional university to the gentler protective mode necessary with adults.

Finding enough time for Open University work seems to have been a universal difficulty, even for those students who have been only too happy to give up many of their previous interests. The 10 hours for 36 weeks confidently predicted in the handbook has evidently been multiplied by two or even three for some students. As one of them wryly says, 'It is just as well I never have to admit the actual number of hours I spend on assignments. I'm sure I'd be told if I take the time I do I should never be taking the course.'

Partly this lengthy and painstaking commitment is due to the care adult students will always take to get their work as exactly right as time will allow. But more importantly, if the optimum amount of work per week has been correctly calculated by the university, the comments of these students do suggest that the main cause of this large extra consumption of time may be loss of familiarity with learning procedures and lack of confidence in manipulating them. If these students are at all representative of a general trend, there would seem to be a role here either for the university itself or for other agencies of adult education to help students use their time more effectively. Partly it is a case of needing simple advice and practice in 'how to study'; partly it is a case of needing actual preparatory material in the subject of the course. More than one of these accounts speaks gratefully of the value of the correspondence courses provided by the National Extension College in conjunction with the BBC which indicated some of the demands and methods a typical Open University course might take. The university has so far been chary of linking its name with any 'preparatory' courses which might suggest either the promise of a place or the need for 'qualifications', but there is clearly a gap for many students between their aspirations and keenness on the one hand and their rusty abilities and academic confidence on the other. If nothing else, there is an entrepreneurial role here for the buccaneering adult education institute principal.

The many sceptical critics of early plans for the Open University were not slow to point out how the inevitable isolation of the lone student would militate against learning success. It seems true that even the carefully nurtured regional organization with its string of study centres and counsellors has not been able totally to make up for the stimulus to learning which full-time higher education gives.

For many students the counsellors, and course tutors and study centres have obviously helped them over the worst of their difficulties. For others, the role of the study centres in particular seems to have been ambiguous. It has to prove an occasion of outstanding merit to make it worth undertaking a long trip over several miles. Mr Ash carefully sums it up in his comments like this: 'Certainly I sometimes feel that I can ill afford the couple of hours fortnightly at the centre, but on balance it does seem worthwhile . . . I am sure that most of us have gained something by mixing and discussing together. Has our study centre failed? It may simply be that the classroom atmosphere of the technical college . . . the lack of easy chairs and coffee facilities do not form an inviting atmosphere.'

However, the real prize for reducing feelings of loneliness and isolation must go to the summer schools. Approached with at least mixed feelings by some and with pure, clear trepidation by many, the summer schools have triumphed for these students where the study centres and counselling-tutorial services have been more diffidently received. Students found the summer school to be 'an exhilarating, if exhausting, experience'; 'It brought the whole thing into focus and I came home even more enthusiastic'; as well as recording an astonishment that the gods of the television programme and the tutor-marked assignment were actually real people who were willing to discuss and drink beer until the small hours. The essence of the pleasure students took in summer schools seems to have been in sharing with others, often for the first time, the pleasure and excitement of intellectual interest in a subject, 'It was during one such discussion that I first appreciated mathematics for what it is, and not the necessary evil I had previously imagined it to be.' Such experiences went a long way with these twenty students towards sustaining them through the periods of loneliness, isolation and lack of confidence which many describe.

There is a limit to the amount the university itself can do and it may be that more important than all the local tutorial services and the summer schools is the way all of these students seems to have found someone to give them direct personal support. Never mind that most of the people they meet socially find it eccentric or incomprehensible that they are OU students. At home or at work they all have someone who is quietly and firmly on their side. In two of the households, both husband and wife have enrolled. Mr Hope, a local government employee, has an exceptionally understanding boss who has found him a friendly local teachers' centre in which to study one day a week. Another student survived her divorce and is carrying on with her degree, drawing support from a secretarial job in an educational environment where her motives and interest are understood.

This is all the more remarkable in the light of the domestic and professional disruption these accounts describe. The Open University may be the first university designed especially for adults, but this does not mean that the work can be done without sacrifice. Holidays are turned over to summer schools, dinghy racing is given up, fiction on library shelves must be ignored in favour of more sober fare, children must learn to cook, be more self-reliant and do without 'Tom and Jerry'. Husbands and wives share out the roles, or sometimes, the day must be lengthened so that domestic life goes on yet more perfectly than before in case anyone complains of neglect.

A place to work and store materials is urgently necessary too. The science kit which arrives so pleasingly in December 'like a Christmas present' is greedy on storage space; a goldfish must be trained for one of the experiments in the 'Biological Bases of Behaviour' course, even in a household which has forsworn pets; all those files, course units, library books and sheets of A4 paper demand a protected area of peace and privacy, not to say a larger letterbox. Mr Hughes has been able to convert an old granary on his farm into a study, and paints an attractive picture of himself surveying his stock, at the same time as he ponders Renaissance art. Other students have evidently exchanged more woeful tales of serious difficulty in finding any quiet, warm place in which to work.

These twenty students record very little discomfiture with the unconventional methods of work the Open University demands. One or two long for lectures, but apart from a not-too-unkindly scorn for CMAS, they seem well-satisfied with the work. Perhaps this is because correspondence combined with the kind of active experimentation most of the OU course units adopt comes near at least one ideal of adult learning—it allows learning at the student's own pace and reduces dependence on short-term memory. What appears at first to be a disadvantage of the correspondence university thus turns out to be an advantage, especially when the course units are so attractively produced and bear no resemblance at all to the dismal duplicated sheets the words 'correspondence course' usually conjure up.

The motives of the student who come forward for conventional adult education are often subjected to intense scrutiny and then pronounced unfathomable. No one could read these accounts from Open University students and be in any doubt about their motives. With the exception of the teachers, they generally have no particular hope of career advancement. Mr McTaggart-Short, approaching his eighties, pungently tells enquirers that he is doing a degree 'to help me get a better job'. Others are equally dismissive of the career motive (though most shrewdly comment that there may well be indirect benefits). With them all, the dominant motive is the wish to prove themselves, to test out what they suspect to be the case—that they have abilities which can be proved against some external and rigorous standard.

Perhaps this strong sense that social and educational justice is at last coming their way accounts for the almost religious fervour and gratitude with which so many students speak of the Open University. They have quickly forgiven and forgotten the misprints in first editions which caused hours of unnecessary extra work, the traumas of the prolonged postal strike, the first inadequacies of the counselling services because they *believe* in the Open University and they have already given it the kind of loyalty which would be derided as old fashioned anywhere else in the educational system: 'We never really lost the delight of being selected, nor the feeling that with all its shortcomings and teething problems, the Open University presented a tremendous ideal, in which we were grateful to be part.'

Students confidently exchange the Open University's very own jargon, speaking without self-consciousness of TMAS and CMAS S100 or D283 and identifying themselves by their student numbers. No wonder, as several point out, the Open University has become for them a way of life.

Part IV

Some students

Chapter 10

Welsh hill farmer

My interest in adult education, on the receiving end, has extended over many years, and has been one of the great pleasures of my life. For the last three winters I have been a member of a very enthusiastic village class (WEA) largely devoted to the work of the remarkable Welsh poet, Bobi Jones.

One of five children, I was born here on this farm in the small village of Bwlchgwyn, in the Denbighshire uplands; went to the village school and the grammar school at Wrexham. Then followed a period of five years in a bank, with war service in the army somewhere in between. The offer, and acceptance, of a farm partnership in West Wales changed the whole course of my life. I eventually gravitated northwards and was fortunate in raising enough money to buy back this farm, which had previously been in the family for at least a hundred and fifty years. I consider myself a very 'run of the mill' farmer, but have enjoyed the last twenty years in country surroundings.

After starting the OU humanities Foundation Course in 1971 my basic ignorance of the arts became manifestly clear to me. The rigour and discipline of a planned course proved to be very different from my previous dabbling, dilettante approach. The wide scope of the course was also an eye-opener. Beginning with the nature of history, I soon sensed that one was cautiously and tentatively skating on very thin ice all the time, a very salutary introduction to all the disciplines. Background reading in some depth was necessary, and still more time needed to 'think hard' about concepts and ideas with which the course units and set books were saturated. I managed to do seven assignments before the seasonal work on the farm forced me to forgo that aspect of the work. My grades had been very satisfactory, and I contented myself with reading the course material only afterwards. Despite this I enjoyed the exam itself: its impromptu nature, demanding spontaneous reactions, was refreshing after the work on the assignments. I feel at fifty-three that my memory is functioning less efficiently than formerly. This year, as a result of conversion of the milk herd into a suckling unit, I hope to have enough time to do justice to the second-level 'Renaissance and Reformation' course.

One course a year is enough for me, and for most people. I mean to enjoy all the courses at a pace that I can stand! My correspondence tutor for the last assignment, not content with giving me an 'A', advises me to be 'more ambitious and prepared to make mistakes'. I take his point. Perhaps he little realizes the care, sweat and blood that preceded my attempt at total comprehension of the theme!

I have converted (with second-hand material from a demolition merchant) an old granary into a study. It overlooks the farm yard and the fields, and enables me to survey the farm and stock. It also provides easy access at opportune times during the day without disturbing the rest of the household. One wall has been decorated with art-plates taken from the course units, so that I am constantly reminded of the eminence and genius of Giotto, Masaccio, Leonardo, Michelangelo, Raphael and others.

My fellow students are a mixed bunch—hospital matron, schoolmasters and health visitor. We are gradually developing a sense of identity with each other, and, somewhat nebulously, with the university itself. In my case a possible degree at the end will be little more than formal recognition that I have survived the test. The fun will have been in the doing. Dare I hope that I can be of more use to myself and to others afterwards? The summer school at Keele last year was my first holiday off the farm in twenty years, and much appreciated. Family and neighbours willingly looked after things in my absence. I returned mentally exhausted, but very pleased with the experience. How I wish we had as extensive a library as Keele's somewhere in the vicinity!

Welsh is my mother-tongue, and I should have liked to do the courses in Welsh. The Open University in Wales must press for this in future. Perhaps I am rooting for a new job in the translations' department!

J. Elwyn Hughes

Chapter 11

Secretary

The first announcement of a proposed 'University of the Air' seemed like a gift from the gods. My husband's work took him away a great deal and both my children were at school. I had an interesting part-time job locally, but I still felt the need to do something constructive with my time. I had taken several evening courses, but the OU seemed to provide the perfect answer.

Just before starting my studies I started divorce proceedings, and my first year as a student was shadowed by the emotionally and financially destructive elements concomitant with this situation. It meant finding a new job, and adjustment to a new way of life where money and leisure would be in very short supply. I was fortunate in getting a secretarial post in the University of London.

My son was fourteen and my daughter twelve when I started my studies, and I shall always be grateful for their willing sharing of the chores. We had to gear our lives to my new job which kept me away from home from 7.30 in the morning till about 7.15 at night, and I knew it wouldn't be easy trying to combine maintaining a home and family relationship, with a full-time job and a course of advanced study. We managed to work out a fairly satisfactory compromise, whereby if I am struggling with completing an assignment, the record player is kept down low, and in return the childrens' friends come in for 'coffee-shop' evenings and I help if I can with homework and other problems that arise. They are sufficiently involved themselves with homework not to be surprised to find me peeling potatoes while reading a book on Renaissance Art.

I gave up dinghy racing, which had taken up most weekends and holidays, learning to play the classical guitar, since I now had no time or money to spare for lessons, practice or concert-going. It meant cutting down my reading-for-fun, and curtailing social activities, though not the total exclusion of old and valued friends. It meant that my holiday was the summer school.

I used the time spent each day travelling for straightforward reading, and learned to accept the curious glances of fellow travellers when they saw I was reading Descartes or Copernicus. On one journey, I was struggling with logic; people peering over my shoulder started arguing amongst themselves as to the solution of the problem. I'm not sure whether this exercise encouraged or discouraged recruits. Nowadays I do my serious studying late at night, from 10 p.m. onwards. One of the compensations of being a 'loner' now is that I can read in bed into the small hours if I choose.

To follow a course of study which necessarily affects and to some extent disrupts normal family life requires a certain amount of ruthlessness on the part of the student, and tolerance on the part of the family. There are the temptations of a good play on television, an evening frittered away reading last week's *Sunday Times*, or just pushing the books to one side and sitting chatting.

Like many mature students, I still have the 'teacher-in-front' hang-up from my own school days, and I often feel I would like more opportunities for face to face instruction. The Foundation level provided weekly study-centre sessions, monthly lectures and a whole residential week at university. The second level came as a rude awakening and I believe that three one-day sessions are a poor substitute, especially in the humanities, where discussion and controversy form the very life-blood of the discipline. I believe that I could have contributed to and gained more from a second summer school than I did even from the first.

There is a certain elitist quality in being an OU guineapig, and doubtless time will charitably cloud memories of misprints in course units, and the postal strikes and power cuts which dogged the early days. For all the problems that have arisen, I have still found myself imbued with missionary zeal, compelled to spread the word. I can claim at least one convert—a taxi-driver whom I met several times over the first two years when I travelled back late from London. Over this period I managed to winkle him out from his firmly held opinions that all education should cease at fourteen, and I recently heard that he has been accepted as a humanities student.

It is difficult to assess what use I shall make of my studies, apart from widening my horizons. I'm not using the course as a means to an end, just to give me a few extra pounds of income when I can tack B.A. after my name. I want to be able really to gain something from these studies which is why I'm only taking one course per year at present. I make no secret of the fact that I am thoroughly enjoying my ou work, though I sometimes get a guilty feeling that 'work' ought not to be fun.

Valerie Saunders

Chapter 12

My hobby

Press announcements giving details of the Open University first drew my attention to the possibility of enjoying a university education and my wife, knowing my predilection for studying in informal ways, thought it would suit me. When the first official intimation was made I wrote for the appropriate literature and read it avidly. I may say that that was the last time I read anything avidly.

In explaining the term 'informal ways', I was tempted to digress into my educational history. That however is a bit like a hypochondriac describing his surgical operation and the normal adult interested in the Open University probably has that kind of educational history.

My 'direct grant' school and I did not agree and at the age of sixteen I left, assured of a good situation as a street-sweeper, such was the school's incompetence.

I thereupon joined an insurance company and passed all the professional examinations, failing practically every subject before passing it. I am inclined to ascribe my successes to good attendance. Being not very intelligent therefore, I decided to bestow my talents on the science Foundation Course. Alternative choices are usually asked for and I put down 'Understanding Society' as a second preference. My reason for the choice of the science course was a desire to learn something about chemistry, to assist me in my work, which is mainly concerned with fire prevention. Once further details of the Foundation Courses were issued and I realized I would actually have to put down a deposit for a 'science kit' I took fright and adopted my second choice. I am so very glad now that I did.

'Understanding Society' is a marvellous mix of disciplines. Having studied it, I now detest economics, know something of politics, feel involved in sociology, am entranced by geography, and can spell psychology. The social sciences are not going to benefit me directly, and I may say I am not likely to benefit them either, but I am thoroughly enjoying studying them.

In 1972 I studied 'New Trends in Geography' and 'The Sociological Perspective'.

The assignments, which are required for continuous assessment of students, do not bother me unduly. That may be why I consistently score low marks. I have an 'F' fail for one TMA. Amongst my fellow students 'F's appear to be non-existent—or are they just not saying? The CMAS pose no great problems. They are not as important as the TMAS, and a lot of unproductive time may be spent on them.

As I said above I am enjoying myself studying with the Open University. This is however disrupting my family life, and restricting many of my other activities. My family find my studying a deprivation, and in view of this and the fact that my studies are unlikely to affect my career beneficially, I will not take it amiss if I am considered selfish. Are we selfish? A moderate golfer will spend much longer on the golf course in his playing life than I will ever spend on my 'transient hobby'.

Michael Gardner

Chapter 13

Married couple

We have always most enjoyed those things which we have been able to do together, and the advent of the o u, which so suited our educational requirements, presented an opportunity to study together which could not be missed.

We were rather dismayed by the colossal amount of correspondence which arrived demanding our attention, and which, together with the course material, threatened to overwhelm us in the first few weeks. We concluded this must be a test of endurance, assessing our staying power.

A way of life has evolved in which we study when we can, without a formal plan. We still enjoy an active social life and have maintained most of our hobbies.

Stan, as manager of a small family engineering firm, can usually arrange some study period during a day in every week, as well as some evenings and weekends. Dinah, trained as a radiographer, now a housewife and mother of two daughters aged six and eight and so both at school, has plenty of time to study during term. School holidays present a problem in that Dinah feels it is unfair to the children and herself to try to study much in the daytime.

There are times when the pressure becomes rather too much and feelings of inadequacy set in, and here the sympathy and support of the other partner are particularly valuable. This helps soften the blow when our labours are returned critically demolished! As this year we are studying a half-credit course, 'Biological Bases of Behaviour', together, this aspect is extended into discussions and appraisals of one another's work.

There is a lot to be said for studying the same subject together, but some things we find best avoided. When TM As and CM As are being first prepared, there must be a total lack of communication with one another (but only on this score!) until the main body of the work is done.

The CMAS are inevitably discussed before they are sent off. The TMAS present a different type of problem. We decided that too much discussion prior to writing up would produce an inevitable sameness about our work which would be obvious to our tutor and detrimental to our individuality. We now find that discussion after initial preparation of a TMA is helpful, and may result in us improving on our original work.

Where the course involves home experiments as in this case, the mutual aid aspect is even more valuable. Our kits are duplicated so we can compare instrument performance, and utilize the other's equipment if necessary. A certain competitive spirit arose in training our goldfish, but when one of them died, all was not lost.

The local study centre gives as much as we require, though we know some students disagree. We feel that primarily the OU has a correspondence function, and the provision of centres and tutorials are necessarily of secondary importance.

We both participate in the activities of our study centre and take delight in meeting people of similar minds to ourselves, albeit most of them teachers, and now number many of them among our personal friends.

Our experience regarding tutorials has been similar, neither of us finding them particularly satisfactory in the first year, but in the second year this aspect has improved greatly, although unfortunately fewer tutorials are available.

The summer school we did not relish prior to the experience, as, doing different courses, we were to be separated for a week. However, each of us left summer school feeling mentally stimulated and stretched, if somewhat tired physically. We are fortunate in that the children have willing grandparents with whom they were delighted to spend this time; the dog, and this year the goldfish, also being extended hospitality.

The children probably did get short shrift in the weeks preceding the exams. They only suffered previously when denied 'Tom and Jerry' due to the university's inept timing of some broadcasts! On the whole they have been remarkably tolerant and slightly amused by our 'lessons'.

The experience of the university has had some effect on developing our personalities. Stan claims to have noticed that Dinah's argumentative ability has not only gained in force, but also she can quote a number of sources to support her assertions. Dinah particularly has gained confidence, Stan having experienced this phenomenon on a previous course in works management.

Stan envisages taking advantage of the broad spectrum of ou courses to expand and revise his knowledge and keep abreast of technological advance, particularly in subjects associated with his career, mainly technology, science and maths, but also enriching his educational background in courses taken for pure interest, such as 'Biological Bases of Behaviour'.

Dinah's motivation is difficult to fathom—for her learning is almost an end in itself—an enjoyable process, but there is also an element of personal challenge. She has always been greatly interested in what goes on inside people (witness her profession). She admits that if the ou had not appeared on the scene, she would probably be an earning part-time radiographer again by now—a point which Stan regards as a definite discredit to the ou!

Stan and Dinah Penman

Chapter 14

Housewife with five children

I am a housewife with five children and I left school at fifteen. I did not want to leave school and a few years ago I started studying with the National Extension College (a correspondence course), and with the help of them and the local technical college collected three 'A' levels in maths and science.

I had been conditionally accepted by Southampton University and was due to start in October 1971 when I heard about the Open University, and I decided that it would fit in with my life with less upheaval. There are various disadvantages in the OU courses for the housewife; work continues during school holidays (with summer schools in the middle of the summer holidays), the television and radio programmes in the early evening and at weekends could hardly be at a worse time, and the tutorial and counselling sessions are, as well, at times when the family is around. These timings are obviously unavoidable and are disadvantages to only a small minority of student-mothers with school-aged children, and the advantage of being able to study when it is convenient and not at specified times compensates for all this; also exams in November are well timed.

I suppose most working mothers suffer to some extent from domestic and maternal bad conscience; I started baking my own bread and doing my own laundry at the same time that I started my OU course. I certainly have not had to make sacrifices in order to do this course (probably because I enjoy the work more than anything I did before). I said as much to my family and got a few morose remarks such as 'sacrifices like giving up mending my trousers'.

The elder children say they are proud of me, which is very gratifying and I can now help them with their SMP-type maths homework which puts me one up on most parents of my

95

generation who were brought up on traditional maths. My younger daughter would rather that I did not work and had more time to spend on them, but I am afraid that if I was not doing this I would be doing something else. My youngest cannot remember my being anything but a student and was very surprised to find that all mothers did not work in a similar way. At least I am home all the time and they know that they can interrupt my work (unless I am watching a programme) and they are all learning to cook. A sympathetic husband is an essential and I have one.

There are disadvantages in being 'founder students'; there is a limited number of higher level courses available for those wanting to do an honours degree; this seems to apply particularly in the maths Faculty. Other things will also improve; the counselling system is a good idea but there seems to be a danger that the wrong people get 'counselled'. The counsellor is told not to be obtrusive or to appear to interfere, but a lot of people who really need help are those that do not go to the study centre for varying reasons, either domestic, health or else are too shy. These are not academic difficulties and they may well be turning in good grade assessments so that the counsellor assumes all is well—but actually meeting other students is invaluable. I do not mean academically (although this as well), but to give a feeling that one is not alone. I know two people who dropped out due to a feeling of isolation. The summer schools are very good value here, different people get out of it different things.

I started out in a slightly worried frame of mind (as, I think, did most of us) about the value of the o u degree; especially what outside opinions would be—one would not want after four/five years of work, to trot up to a prospective employer, o u degree in hand, only to have them fall over backwards with mirth. I think our doubts are being allayed. It seems that the opinion of outside academics is that the standard is if anything above that of traditional universities and we are realizing that probably credit will be given for actually sticking the course—anyone that can do this will show that they possess a certain amount of strength of purpose.

Jill MacKean

Chapter 15

Local councillor

My husband and most of our friends have degrees and I only took a teacher-training course. Maybe I had come to see myself as a domestic cabbage in spite of a part-time teaching post and an active interest in local politics. The four children were growing up and able to be more independent. Finally the type of subject offered by the ou appeared to offer me stimulation and guidance—and allowed me to do it in my own home in my own way.

Having been accepted for the 'Understanding Society' Foundation Course my first problem was how to organize my time to include ten hours' study a week. I taught every morning, so decided to work two hours each afternoon before the children came home from school. This was an excellent scheme in theory! Probably the biggest problem of all was learning to concentrate. Luckily the ou had the good sense to take into account only the best eight of one's first ten assignments: they discount the two worst excesses of elderly new boys and girls.

Once a routine is established it inevitably involves a radical change in the whole pattern of your life. And this doesn't take account of unexpected crises, such as when I was elected as a local councillor. This in itself meant giving up my local teaching job and starting a new one in a different field of education, and also devoting most of my evenings to committee work. The ou had to be fitted into a whole new pattern of life. It meant for instance, that I was suddenly isolated from my study centre, my tutor and my fellow students. Still the impetus remained. I discovered that the Foundation Course was not, in fact, too demanding. And the week's summer school confirmed one's feelings that it was all very much worthwhile. Summer school crystallized the year's work and gave an impetus to flagging intentions. In the

97

event, and in spite of many doubts and misgivings, I passed the crucial first examination.

The second level, inevitably, proved to be more difficult. The two half-credit courses I chose—'School and Society' and 'The Sociological Perspective'—involved a great deal more reading and research than the first year's single and general subject. There was a need not only to understand but to be able to criticize intelligently and constructively. This was an intellectual faculty which had laid dormant during the whole period when I was bringing up a family—and a fairly painful one to resuscitate. There was the further problem that tutors did not always answer letters describing one's own problems and that all too often they returned assignments and comments too late to be really useful. For students who are trying hard, and in isolation, to keep up, this can be very depressing. But despite all this the subject-matter remained both fascinating and involving. New paths of thought were constantly opened, new techniques of investigation con-constantly being suggested. The course material was sensitively designed to help students to economize on time and still do their work intelligently and well.

Such a number of possible paths are open, that one is able to pursue an interest as it materializes. This is one of its major advantages over a conventional university course. At first I had no specific aims, merely a wish to study again. Now I am already finding that quite apart from the broadening of my own intellectual horizons, the work and reading I have done in a year and a half as a student at the o u are becoming useful to me in my work as a lecturer in pre-school education.

Elizabeth Murphy

Chapter 16

Music teacher

For seven of the previous twenty years I had taken extra-mural university courses. At nineteen, editor of a college magazine, I had protested loudly against Latin, Anglo-Saxon and comparative philology being compulsory in an honours English degree course. One failed exam enabled the system smoothly to eject dissidents like me, stamping them 'failed' (and guilty). At the 'university of the second chance' I had a choice of inter-disciplinary foundation courses. Social engagements were cancelled, but new contacts were made with O U regional staff at study centres. Friends were very pleased to see me when I *did* emerge from the study-bedroom. One student's nine-year-old daughter said: 'I think when I go to university, I'll go away. I wouldn't like to be alone in the attic every night like Daddy.'

I admired the courage of lecturers facing alien, ruthless cameras, being fixed on film, with small measures of time for wide topics, working in public before students, critical academics and possibly prejudiced press. Units were splendidly set out, illustrated, and enticing. But tutors who marked assignments were remote. Unseen, they returned essays with a few lines of criticism and gradings which roused roars of astonishment— meetings at the local study centre were explosive after the first batch of essays was returned. Two courses meant two tutors and it seemed that humanities tutors were more responsive, more verbose, than social scientists. O U students had obviously invested much emotional capital in the venture. Essays were compared, grades were compared, tutors were compared, courses were compared, complaints were voiced *fortissimo*, penned *con anima* and Walton Hall certainly had 'feedback'. *Now* tutors meet their students and face-to-face discussion adds value to written work.

The inter-disciplinary approach was more fruitful in some

areas than in others. History pervades all the arts; art, music, and literature reflect their age and society, and so the humanities had a jointed skeleton. The social sciences set out to study 'Man in Society' but seemed multi- rather than inter-disciplinary. Each area of study—economics, geography, political science, demography—had its unique flavour and method of presentation. Each had a slab of time (eight weeks for economics) while sociology and psychology burst in spasmodically to 'apply' themselves, to herd the sheep into one pasture and darn? mend? the holes? (cement the cracks) in the disciplinary texture. They were very welcome, especially the jaunt into the Japanese organization of labour which, for me, alleviated a tough clump of economic curves. Economics, geography and demography strained my maths, my memory, and at times my credulity. They also engendered sympathy for any government trying to untangle national economic problems. Models of land-use, industrial location, profit-maximization, shopping-centre hierarchies, cost-benefit analysis of family-planning programmes, 'person trip' models, showered students with figures and graphs. They frightened those who suffered from figurephobia, but, paradoxically, economics proved intractable to me, although the figures used are friendly tens and twos.

Television's animated charts displayed economists' ideas delightfully and charmed me without convincing me. Geography made a powerful ally of TV although traffic noise and winds competed successfully against the lecturer's voice at times. Sociology had the best of TV. No statistic can compete with the bleak face of the trawlerman as he answers questions about his work. We experienced a little of life on a trawler, life in the Himalayas. I had read sceptically sociological conclusions drawn from investigations where students had been subjects, and experiments had depended on 'stooges' paid to structure the situation—stooges who were students and not professional actors. On TV we saw a social psychologist use an accomplished professional actor in two roles. First he was a 'middle-class gentleman' asking people in Waterloo Station for directions. Then he was a 'working-class man' doing the same thing. Concealed cameras recorded attitudes, psychologists discussed conclusions in the studio afterwards. This was convincing.

Offprints of articles from specialist journals and encyclopaedias gave easy access to important work in psychology and sociology. Photographs brought Harlow's monkeys into focus. The study-bedroom became an Aladdin's cave for the mind and I rarely felt imprisoned. Examination time brought an increase in tension. There were soothing broadcasts to reassure the faint-hearted. It was true that continuous assessment meant I was relatively 'safe' but I still felt I might 'muck it up' at the end of course, and tether. I was still plucking corn in alien fields. I had learnt so much but wondered if it would stay with me, to be a useful tool in argument? I think it has.

Millicent Sherwood

Chapter 17

Older student

Approaching membership of the ranks of sprightly octogenarians,
I am often challenged, out of curiosity or goodwill, 'What do you
want with a degree?' to which, appropriately, I reply, 'To help
get me a better job!' or 'a Freudian wish-fulfilment' or 'Just
satisfaction in achievement'. This disarms them and sometimes
puzzles, but the real truth is that I am taking up the 'second
chance'!

Precluded from going on to grammar school from Board
school, as my siblings did, because of the advent of the first war
and my joining up, there still remained my constantly recurring
dream to burn the midnight oil in rewarding study at residential
college and at long last came the fulfilment in my attending
summer school at that magnificent university seat at Exeter,
writing a TMA of my own choice and choosing philosophy as my
subject. What a nerve! but the joy of getting a 'B', notwithstanding the cryptic caption 'an out-of-the-ordinary essay' needs to be
experienced!

I seem to have been teaching and learning all my life, Sunday
school, training Scouters, school lecturer, army, Naval Cadets
(RNVR), fireguards, wardens, university and college lecturer,
USA productivity study teams, learning the rag trade, trained as
auctioneer and valuer, running an attractive sports and schools
outfitting store, which was blown up in the war.

To get a basic training in university methodology and presentation technique and assessment and the normal style of essay
writing and how to read and use text books, I fortunately took the
'gateway' course of the National Extension College and I cannot
praise it too highly as a preparatory measure.

Reading humanities (A201) and social science (D203) second
level, I find it requires about thirty hours per week; it is impossible

to measure the thought time that one gives to the studies but they are a constant and pleasant, albeit sometimes frustrating, mental activity, with the encouragement of rewards in the offing for the intellectual exercise. Anno Domini creeps relentlessly on, so I am anxious to complete my course within three years, for alas, although I have a curriculum vitae that reads like a pedagogical summary, none of it will qualify me for a credit exemption. Experience and qualifications except from a very restricted source, count for nothing. This is something that ou could usefully look into, notwithstanding the clear cut current academical answer promptly given.

Study centres call forth mixed feelings. The younger group, teachers especially, like them but that group is a decreasing quantity whilst some of the more mature feel that they can make better use of their time. The acid test is as to how many frequent them. I go to maintain touch and sometimes we get a good tutorial. Day and weekend schools and especially the summer schools are quite a different matter and most valuable. The summer schools in famous universities are a first-class institution. Apart from the opportunity of living with people who are doing just the same sort of studies as you, the friendship and understanding makes it a joyous experience for the many who have never lived in collegiate surroundings. There is that wonderful sense of 'belonging'. To meet in person the idols of our fan club, that galaxy of star academicians who, we discover, are so approachable, helpful, encouraging and quite human! They exude a sort of dedication and camaraderie in this great adventure for us on the paths of learning. Mind you, I must confess to a little disappointment that our PROFS and DOCS and DONS didn't at least wear a graduate's gown of some sort in the traditional manner; as an ilk their sartorial inelegancies baffle description but boy, oh boy,! cool your eye! do they know their stuff? and how to put it over? *and* they DO!

My only complain about the ou is 'Why wasn't it started before?' Every so often, in this dear old country of ours, we trot something out of the lucky bag that is imaginative, fills the bill, a touch of genius, and becomes the envy of the world. Such is ou.

Arthur McTaggart-Short

Chapter 18

Perpetual student

Having left school at sixteen in 1930 I have spent many of the years since in resenting that my brother was sent to university and I was not. Beyond reading about two non-fiction books a week I have indulged in no intellectual activity for forty years.

In 1970 I was in a deep rut: self-employed in a small retail business with an intelligent adopted daughter of fourteen who was already better educated than I was. I applied for two Foundation Courses but remain grateful that only science was accepted. S100 has proved extremely difficult and to gain any comprehension of the subjects has been an interesting challenge.

I think the ou could have indicated that some grounding in the various disciplines was desirable. (Had this been done I would never have dared to apply!) However, I know I wasted the months after receiving my acceptance for S100 by not being recommended to study chemistry, physics, biology and maths at least to 'O' level. As it was I tried to learn from some 'self-taught'-type books in these subjects, instead of joining classes. I seemed to believe that new teaching methods would fill in all the gaps painlessly and such (to me) new ideas as ions, electrons, the Periodic Table, isomers, buffers, vectors, energy-force-velocity-speed, and others that the post-war child is familiar with would attain a reality.

Early tutorials in physics gave me nothing. I was too ignorant even to ask any useful questions, but later, as new tutors appeared for chemistry and biology I found an added interest in comparing teaching methods. By now cma and tma results were coming back and it seemed possible that it might be worth continuing with the course. I was coming to terms with a much lower learning capacity than I thought I had. I recognized that I could not hope for a 'good' degree but was hooked on the idea of continuing as an OU member just for the hell of it.

At study centre the tutors I had seen were approaching middle age; at summer school they were nearly all young enough to be my grandsons and they were learning too—that we had problems which did not afflict their normal students. It was interesting to find that these young men were surprised to be thanked for trying to answer my questions; also, occasionally I was thanked for raising a point that had not occurred to them. Tutors straight from university are filled with knowledge and may know many of the answers but they lack the experience to know some of the questions. Many stories have been told of the joys of summer school. The one most appropriate to me is that of a Senior Citizen found weeping on the last night. Like me, he had waited forty years for the experience and had 'never had it so good'.

At a recent discussion on planning future courses some students were astonished when I stated that I was less interested in 'getting a degree' than in being permitted to continue studying a variety of subjects at adult level! I realize that I am probably incapable of passing a third- or fourth-level course (although I intend to try with ecology) but I look forward to attempting at least a half-course a year until the OU rejects me. This would make a vast difference to my retirement—I do not have to face the prospect of becoming a vegetable so soon. It is not yet stated that the OU caters for pensioners, but disabled or other types are acceptable. It might reduce the total of human misery by allowing the old to mingle with the young and middle aged in pursuit of a common objective—knowledge! This innocent occupation might reduce the pressure on beds in mental hospitals.

J. Philpott

Chapter 19

Factory worker

The more people I spoke to at the summer school, the more I realized that I was one of a small minority; where were all the people that had missed out on their education, the people, for whom I thought the o u had been created? The fact was, there were none, or none that I could find. The o u had not got through to the factory floor, and being a factory worker myself I was in a position to observe this. I had never seen any notices pertaining to the o u, nor indeed did the unions seem to have any information about it either.

I want to talk to these factory and shop-floor workers who have still not heard about the o u and indeed anyone else who was thinking of taking up further education, and wondering if they could cope with it. There is no doubt about it, parts of the course are very demanding, and at times very difficult. However, the professors and others who write the course units which you receive through the post are able to communicate sufficiently to enable you to get over the difficult areas of study. Most of your spare time will be taken up with study, but you can regulate this to some degree to suit your own requirements. For those of you who have never sat for examinations before, let me tell you about continuous assessment. You send in your assignment to your course tutor, who marks it and sends it back to you, with any comments which might help you. The marks you receive will be added to your examination marks at the end of the year, and when the time comes to take the examinations you will have collected a large proportion of your necessary marks towards the first two credits; you will also have a good idea of how you will fare in the examinations.

If you have a problem and are wondering how to arrive at a solution, the study centre will be of tremendous help; you will invariably find that other students are having much the same difficulties and that group discussion helps to solve these.

There is one central theme that keeps me studying—I've got a working-class 'hang-up' about not having had a reasonable, to my mind anyway, education. I was brought up in the East End of London, and ten years old when the second world war occurred, and my education from then on was to say the least sparse. It never occurred to children in the area in which I lived to talk about becoming say a doctor or a teacher; we were imbued with ideas of just 'getting a job'.

The ou has given me in just over one and a half years dignity and confidence in myself to pursue my studies and press on to get a degree. I could go on at great length, but if I do it will sound like the Salvation Army!

I have managed to get two people interested in taking the course, people who in my opinion are much brighter than I am, but I had to sell the idea to them. This is what the ou must do if it wants to attract more of the people who are capable of learning, but who never had the chance. As one of the men who work with me said when I told him about the course: 'If you can do it, then so can I'.

Tom Wellman

Chapter 20

Insurance manager

There must be many people like myself who find it increasingly difficult to discuss trivialities or to sit through an evening of television. I'm fifty years old and I don't have as much time to spare as I once had.

When my wife heard about Open University and told me about it, I was immediately interested. Surely here was a chance to be put to the task; to be forced to read serious comment and to learn about people and places without waiting until retirement or leaving a well paid and satisfying job. We decided to enter together for the first year 1971 and were accepted about October 1970. She sees the eventual degree as a help to her career as a teacher but I have no such goal. As the manager of the north-east branch of a life assurance company I already hold my own professional qualification and I am unlikely to get more kudos from a degree.

My wife and I both obtained a credit in first-level humanities last year and are struggling with social sciences this year. Looking back on my first year as a student in o u I see on the credit side the remarkably good correspondence units, some good tuition face to face and a bright and busy week at summer school. We went to Exeter University and found a friendly if impersonal atmosphere. I was educated at a grammar school in Newcastle, an ancient edifice that even in 1937, when I left, looked as if the builders had gone to tea and never returned. To one who associated school with down-at-heel classrooms, and teachers who always taught, usually at the top of their voices, summer school was a surprise. We were allocated into groups of nine or ten and my wife and I found ourselves in the company of a silent male Indian Civil Servant, a voluble female Nigerian Civil Servant, a mixture of ordinary teachers and an extraordinary housewife, well-read, with a brilliant brain and a completely disabled husband. The lecturers were just as new as we were, but on the whole they did a good job. Some were right on top of their subject and taught us a good deal, but others were content to counsel a study group and to prod discussion when it flagged. Discussion groups are often stymied by the presence of one or more characters who love the sound of their own voice. One such student at Exeter wore a hearing aid, and eventually his group told him in no uncertain terms to belt up. Chagrined, he disconnected his aid and sulked for the rest of the session.

Students are represented by committees at each study centre and the enthusiasm of the part-time tutors is only equalled by the apathy of the body of students. At Tynemouth, our study centre, we had just enough students to form a committee during the first year, 1971, and when we tried to bring new students into the fold during 1972, we were met with monumental indifference. The committee serves a number of useful purposes, not least being the rapid spread of information, moans and the occasional bouquets between centres and from centres to the regional office and indeed to that shrine of learning, Walton Hall, via a regional committee.

Personal friends know that my wife and I are students, but occasionally chance acquaintances are told. Some stare, as if we had green hair or a third eye, but most people are vaguely interested, knowing only a fraction of the story. I am enthusiastic and, waving my arms at them, pin them to the wall with verbosity, with praise of the idea. So far I have made no converts. We should convert people, not necessarily to o u but to the general theme of a broader base of thinking.

Jack Mainwaring

Chapter 21

Remote student

The end of six months of homelessness is not the best time to apply for admission to the Open University. With two young sons, no income, and with nearly all hope for a secure future gone, it seemed impossible to make plans for a new life any less disrupted than the old. Had I not been turned down for 'part 3' dormitory accommodation three times in three different towns as being 'unsuitable'?

I am twenty-seven years old, an adopted child brought up in children's homes after the death of my adoptive mother. I married a doctor by whom I have a son and who died in a cholera epidemic while visiting his home in India. I have a second son from whose father I am now parted.

I was considered to be of too high a status for dormitory accommodation and I wanted to know why I was 'different', when I and my children could become destitute. I reasoned in my non-academic way that if I was considered capable of solving my own problems I should be suitable for an OU course.

Eventually I found an isolated East Anglian farmhouse, the owner of which was prepared with some reluctance to let to a woman with children. I was isolated and without other means than from my husband and a weekly allowance from social security to enable us to live independently. Moreover I was in a remote area and isolated from intellectual conversation but rather the centre of some suspicion in the neighbourhood. I had already been granted a place in the Open University and fees were due. I applied to the Education Authority but I was informed that they were not able to pay student fees in such cases. I managed to borrow £10 and was able to get work on the land—hard work under dreadful conditions. Meanwhile I had received the first units for two Foundation Courses (arts and social science). But

Walton Hall were coping with the effects of the postal strike and their computer had 'cut me off' as my fees were late. No more units arrived until March. Evening visits to a study centre were impossible as there was no public transport and no one to look after my children. I was able to get one lift with a workman going past the study centre, 25 miles away.

The crisis came when my health broke down and I was admitted to hospital. This looked like the end of university education for me but my counsellor after visiting me in hospital went to the Local Education Authority and asked that they should, in the light of the work I had completed and which the ou had accepted and graded, consider the question of a grant. Eventually it was agreed that I should be one of the few cases for which an exception would be made. By June I was able to borrow all the set books that I needed from the nearest public library, a few miles walk and a 7-mile bus journey away.

The biggest hurdle of all was looming near, the two weeks of summer school. My wardrobe consisted of wellingtons, wooden sandals, jeans, sweaters and skirts. My circumstances were by now known to Walton Hall and I am ever grateful that a hardship fund has been established from which a grant was made for extra clothing and study materials. Adequate clothing and three square meals a day did literally make my hair curl and I was comfortable and relaxed enjoying myself to the full in conversation with tutors and students. Summer school taught me some of the most important aspects of scholarship, positive judgment, objectivity and the rewards to be gained from having an open mind.

It took me five weeks to unwind and order my confused mind after the intensive study of summer school. While there I thought I had learned very little; but home again, with time to reflect, new aspects of a solution or of information from the summer school kept coming to mind and would not settle until it had been thought out. Having tasted the luxury of having a tutor readily available, I decided that no good student should be without one. I wrote to the regional office to point out that as I couldn't get to a study centre and as my essays were marked by many different tutors (fortunately the system has now changed), would it be possible to be attached to one near enough to talk to? My senior counsellor arrived with my D100 staff tutor.

How I ever got to the examination room at the end of the

academic year in November is beyond the comprehension of any but members of the o u. I would have tried to find some way to avoid the occasion if I had still felt isolated. As it was my tutor arrived to look after my children during the first day's examination and my counsellor had found a welfare agency to care for them on the second day. But I still came away from the exam centre shattered.

It was my seven-year-old, who came to my bedroom far too early one morning stating 'your exam results are here, mum'. I buried my head under the pillows and dragged the envelope with me further into the bed while the younger son and the pup lined up for the dreaded moment. I don't remember actually reading of my successes in passing both papers, but just feeling the pain as the tensions relaxed. My sons had played their part in enabling me to study and it was only at this point that I realized how much my success meant to them.

It was not like this with others around me. 'You would be better earning more money than wasting time on those books', was a typical comment from neighbours. Quite recently even a tutor, discovering that I was held up by not being able to afford all the setbooks, wondered aloud (in front of a class) why people in such a position wasted their time in trying to get degrees. Last week in the village store I remarked that it would be of benefit to many villagers if there were some paving stones at our muddy bus stop. The chairman of the parish council heard of the suggestion and took the trouble to come round to my house to ask why, if I was so keen on 'town facilities', I didn't go and live in a town. I am beginning to see the social science in those paving stones and in my teacher's impatience.

Barbara Abraham

Part V

Teachers and courses

Chapter 22

Divide and teach:
The new division of labour

Francis Castles

Lecturer in Government

One always has some expectations about a new job. Mine, when I arrived at the Open University early in 1970, were that it would differ from the sort of institutions in which I previously taught (the University of York and the Australian National University) largely because one's contact with students was indirectly through the media rather than directly in the class-room. But a few months at Walton Hall convinced me that the distinctiveness of the teaching situation stems from the sheer complexity and size of the o u teaching system.

Instead of one relatively undifferentiated group of academics carrying out all the tasks involved in an undergraduate education, the Open University has led to an increasing specialization of role. There are at least four crucial functions performed by academics at conventional British universities in their relation-ships with students. They are providers of information, in lectures and classes and to somewhat lesser extent tutorials. In tutorials they also carry out a second task—the development of students' critical powers. Third, they direct their students' process of learning, and provide an atmosphere conducive to intellectual work. Last, the academics help to introduce the students into the culture of the university. In conventional universities all these functions are carried out by every academic. In the Open University they are largely separated, becoming the full-time responsibility of different groups of individuals.

A headquarters group of academics at Walton Hall look after the provision of information. This obviously presents a problem of feedback—no resonant snores from the back of the lecture hall, no complete incomprehension in tutorials. The academics must rely on the specialized help of educational technologists, who can advise on how information should be presented, and sometimes test material before it goes out to students. Once material is completed, alterations are dependent on an elaborate scheme of monitoring of students' work. In both cases, the replacement of intuitive kind of feedback by a highly explicit external one can lead to tension, as academics can feel that the processes interfere with their exclusive prerogative to decide what should be taught and how.

The techniques of communication used by the Open University also need specialized skills, and lead to similar tensions. In any task needing division of labour it is important to have a clear delineation of spheres of responsibility. This usually comes from trial and error over a period of time. The relationships between the BBC and the academic members of the university is defined as an 'educational partnership'. The academics provide information for students, the broadcasters convey it. Suspicion and conflict can sometimes arise when the BBC producer urges one approach on media grounds and the academic urges another on intellectual grounds.

The university appoints outside experts to advise on the suitability for publication of much of the Open University's academic output. While such collective responsibility ensures against lazy preparation it introduces the possibility of conflict between academic and academic. Whereas the academic profession has always encouraged criticism of published research, teaching has been regarded as a private matter. But, at the Open University, the course team is encouraged to provide constructive criticism. Since the line between constructive and destructive comment is at best a tenuous one, bitter disputes are sometimes engendered in the context of course team discussion. Collective responsibility also brings with it an enormously increased work-load. If course team material goes out under the collective *imprimatur*, each individual involved tends to feel that he should have some control over content. This control can only come from meticulous initial planning of courses, a lot of time spent in reading colleague's drafts, and a prolonged collective discussion of each piece of completed work. Such activities can dominate one's horizons for weeks and months at a time to the exclusion of all other concerns.

Utilization of the mass media makes courses available to huge numbers of students, but cannot greatly develop students' critical ability. The Open University offers students local tutorials as an arena in which course materials can be critically examined. The theoretical problem here is of increasingly formal bureaucratic coordination. British universities have, within a framework of essential administrative rules, usually assumed that rational social organization will happen through the relatively uncontrolled actions of rational beings. How the teacher approaches his teaching for instance has been a matter of individual choice rather than administrative formula. This has been made possible, in large part, by the relative smallness of the teaching institution.

But with many hundreds of part-time tutors, for the most part personally unknown to the central academic staff, the Open University must procure some minimum standardization of the academic content of tutorials, while at the same time preserving some freedom in the choice of teaching methods to encourage the development of an independent critical intelligence in students. Much depends here on the quality of the part-time staff appointed, but inevitably tutors, like the students they teach, are bound to experience in varying degrees a feeling of academic isolation. Because they are caught up in their full-time occupations, and because they are at a distance from the information providers, the Open University has had to devise ways of ensuring that academic objectives are fulfilled. Staff tutors have been appointed full-time, largely to handle these problems; the risk here is the one always encountered in hierarchies—that co-ordination will stifle initiative in the regions. Obviously, this situation makes the staff tutor's position a crucial and difficult one.

Students of universities are not only there to master a relevant discipline but also to learn how to learn. In conventional universities, academics foster this largely by example and by pragmatic advice to students. At the Open University this task too becomes specialized in the hands of a group of full-time senior counsellors and part-time counsellors. In setting up the university it was felt that the problems faced by OU students would be much greater than those of ordinary university students and would consequently require specialist attention. Part-time counsellors have to attempt to overcome the unfriendly academic atmosphere and to try and prevent dropout by rapidly diagnosing and treating problems which arise from circumstances other than academic incompetence.

Conventional university students live in a special world, where the academic task is a major preoccupation of corporate life. But an OU student earning his own living cannot be similarly cut off from the everyday world. Even the university's study centres are almost invariably parts of other institutions on loan, as much part-time as the students themselves. In these circumstances the task of introducing the student to the culture of the university is perhaps the most difficult of all. To some extent, the study centres may serve to provide a kind of academic community on a minor scale. Frequently, they possess a variety of audiovisual devices, and where students have been encouraged to watch university programmes, at least occasionally, as a group, some sort of pseudo-lecture experience has been created.

A major Open University effort to integrate students into the academic community has been the one-week summer schools which are an integral part of each Foundation Course, and which are used by some faculties at second and subsequent levels. One of the few conditions of entrance to the Open University is a commitment to attend such schools—and for a busy individual with limited holidays and/or school-age children this is no mean sacrifice. Summer schools take place at a number of conventional universities in the summer vacation, and again involve a specialized part-time teaching staff appointed for the purpose. While central academic staff and staff tutors do attend for a fortnight each year, the huge numbers of students involved means that their contribution is relatively small.

The faculties design their summer schools to provide a serious load of informational content and to provide opportunities for sharpening critical abilities, but experience suggests very strongly that it is in the context of summer schools, if anywhere, that the student will acquire some sort of corporate identity as part of a community of learning. Certainly, as the person responsible for organizing social science summer schools in 1971–2, I felt (and this feeling was confirmed by the comments of the vast majority of students and part-time summer school tutors) that it was in this context that students came to see themselves as something more than independent learners wearily ploughing a solitary path through the fields of academia.

It is evident from all that has been said that the massive division of labour implicit in the Open University creates a number of problems for student and academic alike. The former is surrounded by a plethora of specialized roles, whose respective functions may in the early days be difficult to comprehend. The latter is shorn of many of the functions to which his role as an academic in conventional institutions of learning may have accustomed him. None the less, role specialization is a concomitant of the division of labour which makes the Open University possible at all. To the extent that one judges the Open University to be a worth-while innovation in British higher education, one must accept the consequences of this division of labour, although not necessarily the particular forms it has taken in the early years of the university.

Chapter 23

The OU academic

Graeme Salaman and Kenneth Thompson
Lecturer in Sociology and Senior Lecturer in Sociology

The occupational ideology of university teachers contains a rather confused self-image of their role. The image is confused for a variety of reasons—one important reason being that the occupational ideology masks differences over interests and values as held by various sections of the profession (scientists and non-scientists, junior lecturers and professors, expansionists and conservatives). Another reason, which is relevant for understanding the position of the Open University academic, is that the occupational ideology of university teachers also depends upon *ex post facto* rationalizations called forth by the need to adjust to changed circumstances.

The increase in student numbers, the changed social composition of the student body, the problems of motivating students to learn when there is no certainty that such learning will bring suitable job opportunities, these are just some of the factors that have brought the academic role under stress. Over the long term the main change has been that the traditional university function of rounding off the preparation of a small elite to step into leadership positions in society has come into conflict with the demand for mass higher education. The old image of the teacher–student relationship was that of a face-to-face, personal relationship, epitomized by the one-to-one tutorial situation. The tutor communicated not just specialized knowledge, but also a whole subculture (that of the cultivated gentleman). In practice, of course, the different strands of the teaching process have long been subject to a division of labour, such as lecturing, tutoring and examining. Oxford and Cambridge have been just as ready to divide the functions as have the large civic or state universities in Britain and America. Because the Open University's students are non-resident adults, the differences between them and conventional university students were explicitly recognized, and, therefore, it was easier to make explicit changes in the academic role by subdividing its functions. In some respects this places the OU academic in a favourable position by resolving some of the role conflicts that face his colleagues in conventional universities.

Like members of other professions, academics believe in the value and necessity of their being free from interference in the execution of their occupational tasks, as they see them. Despite the obvious unreality of this value in many instances and occasions (and despite the fact that academics themselves tend very often to lose interest in this 'value' when there are research funds being offered), there is an important sense in which it can be argued that, for the academics themselves, autonomy is a highly salient value when it comes to teaching. The academic in an ordinary university is free from interference in or control over what he says in his lectures, because his colleagues simply don't know what he's saying. The students, of course, can vote with their feet. When it comes to lectures academics respect their colleagues' privacy: although of course, when it comes to published work they replace colleagueship by competition.

At the Open University privacy is replaced by total visibility: all members of the course team know what the others are writing. Autonomy is replaced by control: members of the course team, and the chairman in particular, have a clear interest in the quality of each member's contribution. This introduces numerous difficulties: not only are the criteria by which to judge academic work open to dispute, but the very activity of judgment itself, in a face-to-face context, is highly unusual, except in a clearly hierarchical academic relationship (for example, a Ph.D. examination or a job interview). Obviously there are considerable possibilities of resentment and bitterness in such a situation. But there's another side to this story. Course teams require colleague control because of the necessary interdependecne of the members and their contributions: but interdependence also means that any individual member of the course team could, if he wished, drastically damage the course by his refusal to co-operate, or by his inefficiency or incompetence.

The position of 'course team chairman' is an interesting feature of the organization of the course team system. The chairman is finally responsible for the appearance, content and level of the course, and its presentation, on time and at a suitable level. The chairman of a course is not necessarily the professor of the main discipline; and, academically, he is very much more important than the professor, for he is the person who represents that course in its dealings with outside bodies, universities, critics and contributors. The position is an important and powerful one, and yet it may be filled by relatively junior members of staff—ordinary lecturers for example. This means that the Open University offers a far greater degree of influence, responsibility and authority, at lower levels within the academic career hierarchy, than other universities.

Another aspect of the rather unusual distribution and location of power and influence at the Open University, is evident in the relationship between course teams and outside academics. OU courses involve outside assistance of many kinds. Most courses employ consultants—experts in the field—to advise, and criticize early drafts of the course. They employ outside academics to assist in the production of, or to appear in, radio and television programmes. They use published and unpublished work, articles, and research reports in editing their custom-built course Readers (which are also on general sale), and they employ academics as part-time tutors and summer school teachers. All this can be seen as a considerable flow of patronage from the course team to their colleagues in the traditional branches of the academic world, involving publicity, status and money. This patronage has obvious implications for the position of the Open University *vis-à-vis* other academics. It also has implications for the members of the course teams, especially the junior ones, who may find themselves with a gift of patronage and influence that would be unheard of elsewhere.

Furthermore the Open University has a number of implications for the professional reputations of the academics. On the whole, academics make reputations and money and get jobs through quantity and quality of their publications; teaching is, because it is invisible and unmeasurable, less important. But, at the Open University, teaching is published as beautifully produced and widely marketed units. The quality of these teaching units, by virtue of the amount of time, money, attention and thought devoted to them, is high. They are often the equivalent, at least, of available textbooks, and may well be used as such. Also since many of the courses produce their own Readers, members of the course team find that they have a ready-made source of publications. It might not be too much to claim that the Open University could be regarded as a licence to make a reputation, especially when it is remembered that OU academics are at the forefront of educational advance and technology, *and* actually appear on the television. What more can any academic want?

But, as we've suggested, things are not entirely rosy. The conflict between traditional academic values and the course team control and interdependence remains, and will certainly become, if it is not already, a bone of contention in some course teams. And some people still regard the Open University as a second-class university. This preconception is based to a large extent on the fact that the OU is equated with correspondence courses. But this view ignores the other strands in the university's teaching system—tutorials, summer schools, radio and television. Taken in isolation, the correspondence material element seems to be the equivalent of the *minimizing* approach to teaching which is so much at odds with the *maximizing* approach advocated by most university teachers. The maximizing approach asserts the ideal of higher education as being mind-expanding without limit or constraint. The minimizing approach settles for a policy of getting students through their courses with a minimum of effort from all concerned. This is a sensitive issue for academics who often find themselves lapsing into minimizing practices, due to pressures from increasing student numbers, students' instrumental attitudes, the desire for good results by departments and by the university itself, and the teachers' own need to do research and to publish. Such pressures have led teachers to concentrate on getting students through examinations, and to fulfilling their teaching obligations with a minimum of effort. The correspondence element in the OU system might be seen as promoting just such a tendency.

But not only does this ignore the teaching functions of the regionally based tutors and counsellors, it also fails to take account of the *maximizing* approach to teaching which provides the *raison d'être* of the radio and television programmes. In many courses the reasonably able student could fulfil the minimum requirements for securing a credit without paying much attention to the broadcasts. But, just as the conventional university teacher could hope to inspire his students in the tutorial, so the Open television can inspire students to look beyond the final examination.

The use of the broadcasting media, and the association with the BBC helps to offset some of the more invidious connotations of the correspondence element in the Open University's teaching system. This has been useful in the early years of the experiment, but it should become a redundant consideration as the effectiveness of the Open University's methods become accepted and it comes to be regarded as a logical development of the various components of traditional university education. And only then will the role of the OU academic be regarded as a natural development of the various elements of the traditional role of university teacher. Until then Open University academics will probably have to rest their claim to acceptance among their more conventional peers on their own individual reputations for research and teaching which they established independently of their present positions.

Chapter 24

Course production at the OU: Basic problems and activities

Brian N. Lewis

Deputy Director, Institute of Educational Technology

Initial expectations

In the earliest days of the OU, before course production actually began, most academics were decidedly optimistic about the ease with which courses could be produced. For example, it was widely believed that, during the first year of course production (1970) a group of eight or nine academics—along with a handful of expert advisers and assistants—would have little difficulty in producing a full 36-week Foundation Course. It was recognized that a great deal of written material would have to be produced. But there was a tendency to perceive this particular task as requiring little more than the imaginative brightening up of already existing lecture notes and professional papers.

Indeed, many academics confidently expected the business of course production to occupy not more than 100–120 days of each calendar year. Most academics took up their appointments on the explicit understanding that they would have time for at least some of the more significant knowledge-extending activities— postgraduate supervision, private research, professional writing, consulting, conference attending, and the like. The OU was to be a *real* university, not just a production house for the development and dissemination of undergraduate course materials.

The harsh reality

These expectations were rapidly shown to be sadly inaccurate. In the first place, nobody had fully thought through the numerous implications of requiring academics to work together in large co-operative teams. Second, no one had fully pursued the implications of having to teach a heterogeneous population of students who were mostly trying to study in their spare time (and

125

perhaps for the first time) and in the isolation of their own homes. To cut a long story short, it soon became obvious that in order to (a) produce effective teaching-at-a-distance materials, and (b) to have time to spare for the various other activities in which academics normally engage, the overall staffing of the OU would ideally have to be increased by a factor of at least 3 or 4. The OU budget would not permit such an increase so a number of compromises and sacrifices had to be made.

In an attempt to establish high teaching standards with too little staff, both the academic and the non-academics have, for example, forgone substantial periods of holiday and study leave. They have also cut their private research activities to the barest minimum in order to devote themselves almost exclusively to the business of course production. At the same time, the rate of production of new courses has been slightly diminished so that the courses which *are* produced stand a better chance of doing an effective job of teaching.

As a result of taking these steps, the production of quality courses is now merely difficult, rather than impossible. But the conditions of service for OU academics (and for many of the supporting staff) must be among the worst in the country. There is still an exhausting rush against time to produce high quality materials. And the pressure is likely to continue for at least five to ten years—the time that it will take to establish a solid stock of well-validated courses.

The size of the problem

The planning and production of correspondence materials, home experimental kits, students' activities, multiple-choice tests, radio and television programmes and the like, make demands on staff which are unlike anything they have ever experienced before. For example, special care must be taken to ensure that each correspondence unit is a coherent and memorable piece of exposition. There must be no mistakes, non sequiturs, gaps or other defects in the argument. All written materials must be self-explanatory and pitched at the right level of difficulty.

The whole operation is extremely time consuming. If an academic wants to write a really effective piece of exposition— one that will either stand on its own or serve as essential supplementary reading to a prescribed textbook—it could easily take him as much as two to three weeks to produce an adequate draft. His first draft would then need to be tried out, along with some appropriate tests, on a representative sample of potential students to see whether it achieves what the author wanted it to achieve. Feedback data from these students can then be used as a basis for revising the original draft, and for polishing it up into more final form. Ideally, the revised draft should *also* be tested (preferably on a different representative group of volunteer students) to make sure that the revision process has been effective, and has not inadvertently introduced further defects and obscurities. In fact, the test-revise-retest cycle should be repeated as many times as is necessary to satisfy the author (and his colleagues) that the correspondence unit really does teach. However, each new cycle can add at least three or four weeks to the overall production time.

In addition to writing the basic correspondence unit, the author must devise appropriate homework assignments. If the homework is to be marked by computer, he must specify *exactly* the marking scheme the computer must use. At the very least, he must say how many marks must be added for each correct answer, and how many deducted for each wrong answer. And he may request the computer to provide him with some detailed information on differential patterns of right and wrong answers.

If the homework is to be marked by correspondence tutors, the author must provide these tutors with appropriate guidelines. And he must tell the computer how to handle the marks or grades that these tutors eventually award. Since the tutors may often be called upon to explain points of difficulty, the author must also circulate adequate briefings on the overall aims and objectives of his units. In some cases, he may wish to provide the study centre tutors with special discussion materials. And he may want the students to perform experiments, or engage in certain kinds of group activity or field work. All of these activities ideally need to be put through the test-revise-retest cycle to make sure that they are unambiguously clear and likely to have the effects intended.

The preparation of concomitant radio and television programmes is no less arduous. Administrative and financial constraints make it difficult to put these programmes through a test-revise-retest cycle, so even greater efforts must be made to ensure that they are right first time. Experience has shown that even the simplest looking programme can take several weeks to plan and produce—especially if it has to be carefully integrated with the correspondence materials, or if anything out of the ordinary (e.g. a special sequence of visual effects) is required.

Some organizational difficulties

To obtain a preliminary insight into the practical difficulties of course production, let us consider a situation in which nine academic members of staff (call them A1, A2 ... A9) agree to collaborate on the production of a 36-unit course. To simplify the initial discussion, we shall focus solely on the problem of producing 36 correspondence units. And we shall suppose that each academic agrees to write just 4 out of the 36 units. As a further simplification, we shall assume that A_1 agrees to write units 1–4, and A_2 agrees to write units 5–8, and A_3 agrees to write units 9–12 and so on.

After several weeks of joint discussion on the aims and objectives and content of the course, the academics go away and start writing. If we accept the kinds of time estimates mentioned earlier, and if we assume that each academic writes his units in numerical order, it follows that after a lapse of a few weeks the first *in extenso* drafts of units 1, 5, 9 ... will be nearing completion. Unfortunately, this natural-looking arrangement rules out the possibility of testing the draft units, in a systematic manner, on volunteer students. Unit 1 can, of course, be tested. But unit 5 can be meaningfully tested only on students who have worked through units 1–4. And units 2–4 have not yet been written.

This is a very considerable difficulty. If the academic members of staff are trying to achieve good continuity from one unit to the next, A_2 might have written his unit 5 as a follow-on to what he *expects* to appear in units 1–4. For example, A_1 might have said that his units 1–4 will introduce some basic concepts in statistical analysis. In preparing unit 5, A_2 will therefore feel free to build upon the statistical knowledge that he believes A_1 will impart in units 1–4. In so far as A_2 takes this statistical knowledge for granted, his unit 5 will be largely unintelligible to the volunteer student who has previously seen only unit 1. Difficulties of this kind tend to increase over successive units. A_5, who has bravely agreed to do units 33–36, is engaging in a tremendous act of faith if his unit 33 tries to build upon, or summarize, material that 8 different colleagues have not yet written.

Should A_2 send off his completed unit 5 to the Media Production Department, with the request that it be set up and printed? If A_2 does this, he will place A_1 under a strong moral obligation to work into his remaining units (2–4) all the knowledge that unit 5 has taken for granted. If A_1 now refuses to co-operate (claiming, for example, that A_2 misunderstood what he, A_1, had undertaken to do), then unit 5 will be partly unintelligible unless expensive alterations are made at the galley proof stage. And A_2 is likely to feel that A_1 has let him down. At the same time, A_2 will have only 3 units left (namely, units 6–8) in which to accommodate to the demands of A_3 and other colleagues. Instead of arranging for units 1, 5, 9 . . . to be printed without further delay, it is tempting to stack them away on a shelf so that they can be altered, if necessary, at a later date. As more units come off the assembly line, everyone gets a clearer idea of what his colleagues are trying to say. Earlier units can then be taken off the shelf (so the argument goes) and adjusted to harmonize with the later ones.

However, it is a mistake to suppose that the mutual adjustment of units becomes easier as more and more units are produced. (As time goes by, most academics become clearer and firmer about their aims and objectives—and this tends to make them *less* willing to alter direction in order to accommodate to the wishes of their colleagues.) Moreover, the retention of units leaves the Media Production Department with almost nothing to do at the beginning of the writing year, and with almost everything to do at the end of the year. To provide the Media Production Department with a steady flow of work, each academic may have to finalize his first unit before he has even started to write detailed *in extenso* drafts to his follow-up units.

In practice, the situation often seems to be less serious than it really is. For example, it is open to each academic to dash off rough outline drafts (of 1,000 words or so) of all 4 units, and to circulate these among his eight colleagues. It is difficult to respond to such material. There tends to be rather a lot of it. And, because of its tentative nature, harsh or detailed criticism always seems to be out of place. There is patently nothing 'final' about the rough outlines produced—and everyone tends to think that, when the time, comes, he will have very little difficulty in accommodating to the wishes of his colleagues. Unfortunately, these hopes are rarely justified. When the time comes, it may be very difficult indeed to adjust to one's colleagues in a satisfactory way. In some cases, an academic may even cite his first outlined raft as 'evidence' that certain proposed adjustments are unreasonable. 'If you wanted me to incorporate *that* sort of material into my unit, you should have made your requirements weeks ago'.

This kind of comment is made in perfectly good faith. At the root of all these difficulties is the failure to communicate intentions and requirements. However well-meaning and co-operative the nine academics may be, they habitually fail to see, in the first instance, the *force* of the points that their colleagues are urging. For example, A_1 might fondly imagine that he can meet the requirements of A_2 by adding a sentence here, a footnote there, and a paragraph somewhere else. In reality, the knowledge that has been pre-supposed in unit 5 might, if taken seriously, call for a radical restructuring of units 1–4, By the time A_1 realizes this, it is too late to do anything about it. And unit 5 will therefore be building on skimpy and inadequate foundations.

Instead of using outline drafts as a first basis for communicating intentions and requirements, it might be thought that longer drafts (e.g. of 5,000 words or so) would be more appropriate. This is not the case. Longish drafts, when produced in a hurry, tend to be discursive tours around the kinds of topics that the writer is *hoping* to cover, just as soon as he gets down to the business of writing seriously. When the serious writing begins, the inadequacies of each person's first thoughts will become apparent. Certain topics will be dropped, others will be introduced, alterations may be also made to improve the structure. It follows that these drafts do not deserve to be taken too seriously.

If long drafts *are* produced, chaos may ensue. Accusations will be made that certain colleagues are planning to pack too much material into their units. Suggestions will be made that the whole course needs to be 're-thought', and that the order of presentation of certain units should be changed. A deeper problem arises if some academic members of staff fail to understand each other's subject matter. If A_3 and A_2 come from different disciplines, A_3 may do his best to make helpful suggestions to A_2— but his comments may nevertheless strike A_2 as being naïve and irrelevant.

It is irksome to have to read so much material, especially if everyone believes (a) that it is going to be radically changed, and (b) that it fails to do justice to the potential abilities of the writers. It can also provoke endless worries and arguments. In this respect, the breathless activity of writing, circulating, and re-writing does *not* lead to a rapid convergence of opinion. The procedure is not self-correcting.

Constraints of time and money

It may be thought that all the main difficulties could be avoided by forward planning techniques. Careful planning can help list the nature of the operation, and the time pressure under which everyone is working, are such that planning cannot possibly solve (or even foresee) all the problems that can arise.

Suppose, for example, that the academics decide upon pre-scribed background reading materials. The most economic way of getting such materials to the students is to arrange to have them published, on the open market, as a Reader in paperback form. However, it takes time to negotiate with publishers. And it takes time to select the contents of the Reader, to secure copyright clearances, to agree editorial changes with the original author and publisher, to insert editorial comments and summaries, to arrange for the whole volume to be set up, proof-read, printed and distributed. The entire venture is impossible unless arrangements to publish are put in hand in the very first quarter of the writing year. Thus academic members of staff cannot have their Reader unless they are prepared to finalize its contents well before most of their correspondence units have been written. This is a frus-trating situation which no amount of forward planning can satisfactorily resolve. In the course of writing a unit, it often becomes clear that the chosen Reader material is not after all the most suitable choice.

In addition to time pressure, the Open University is also labouring under severe economic constraints. If money were less of a problem, academic members of staff could afford, for example, to drop the idea of hurriedly concocting a one-volume Reader. They could arrange instead for the last minute inclusion (in the student's correspondence package) of carefully selected off-prints. Such an arrangement would give them more time **to** select the best possible background reading material. But the *cost* would be very much higher.

Even now, we have touched on only a few of the many background pressures and irritations that academic members of staff encounter. Moreover, our discussion has been grossly over-simplified. In practice, academics do not normally agree to write just four successive units. Instead they want to be involved in the entire course—writing one or two units here, and a few more there. Quite often, they want to write more than they have time to write—and each may feel that his ration of the course is too small to enable him to do a worthwhile job.

Different academics have different working methods, and different views of the educational enterprise. One might be enthusiastic about computer-marked objective tests, whereas another might deplore them. One academic might prefer to write in a friendly and egalitarian manner, whereas others might adopt an impersonal approach. There are literally dozens of ways in which differences of approach and opinion can arise.

Organizational aids to efficiency

The foregoing account is probably a minimal statement of the main difficulties and pitfalls associated with the production of ou course materials. There are many additional difficulties of a more specialized and less obtrusive kind (Lewis, 1971, 1972). An important point to bear in mind is that almost every decision that is made can have hidden and unexpected implications. Because of the constraints under which the ou is operating, there is neither time nor money to indulge in trial and error experimentation. If the right decisions are not made at the right times, production plans may be held up and the quality of the course materials will suffer.

One way of easing the burden is to employ a variety of judiciously chosen assistants. It is helpful, for example, to have assistants who can engage in literature searches—locate background reading materials and suitable illustrations for proposed correspondence units. There is also a need for people who can handle copyright problems, and who can help to co-ordinate the diverse activities in which different members of staff are likely to be engaged at any given time. In addition, there is a need for more specialized assistance in the form of editors and designers and artists—people who proof-read, and advise on problems of format and layout, and create special purpose illustrations and so on. Finally, there is an all-pervasive need for professional advice on the overall strategy and tactics of the whole operation. Within its limited resources, the o u has in fact secured a modest number of assistants and advisers of the kind required. It has also established its own Institute of Educational Technology to advise on the design and evaluation of the teaching materials that are produced and to make recommendations that will help the university to become a rapidly self-improving system.

What else can be done to facilitate the planning and production process? Well, there are some rather obvious precautionary measures that production teams can take. For example, most teams find it convenient to organize themselves, at an early stage, into *small working groups* of three or four members. Within each working group, a member may have primary responsibility for writing a particular set of correspondence materials (or for preparing a particular set of broadcast materials), and the other members have mainly an advisory or watching role. As a further safeguard, the working groups overlap in their membership—so that everyone can function as the main author in some of the groups, and as an adviser or observer in other groups. It follows that each academic can remain in close contact with those colleagues (those writing adjacent units, for example) whom he is most likely to have to accommodate.

There are, however, quite severe limits to what this kind of arrangement can achieve. It is easier to detect disparities of approach than to decide what should be done about them. (Imagine, for example, the difficulties that can arise if three scientists, in overlapping working groups, all start to write in different ways about 'theories and models'.) The setting up of overlapping groups also tends to produce only localized, rather than extended, continuity. There is still a danger of conceptual drift occuring from one sequence of units to the next. To secure some sort of macro-control over the whole 36 units it helps to have an overall chairman and arbiter who is a generalist—in the sense of being able to span the various disciplines of his colleagues —and who also has the knowledge, vision and charisma to keep everyone moving in the same direction. Needless to say, this is easier said than done.

Some recent developments

In recognition of the very real difficulties that arise when teams of a dozen or more experts collectively try to produce a full course of up to 36 weeks' duration, several attempts have been made in recent months to simplify matters. One popular strategy has been to abandon the quest for close-knit overall integration, and to divide courses into several self-contained blocks of 4–8 units each. This enables everyone to work in much smaller groups and to worry much less about what their colleagues are producing in *their* blocks. A similar ploy consists in producing half-courses and third courses (and even one-sixth courses) of no more than 18 or 12 (or 6) units each. In addition, the original aim of generating 36 weeks' work (in respect of each full course) has been widely modified to a less gruelling 30–32 weeks' work. This reduces the work-load on the course teams, and gives the student a very welcome week off, here and there, in which to catch up or revise, or just rest.

Several other simplifying strategies exist. There is, for example, an increasing tendency to rely more heavily on already-existing texts—instead of trying always to create special new materials from scratch. In view of the clash of viewpoints and styles that can arise when different academics each contribute to a common course, some academics have also agreed to hand over the main writing chores to just one or two like-minded colleagues. This means that, for one course, just one or two academics will take responsibility for the bulk of the writing, the remaining academics acting as their assistants throughout. In subsequent courses, the roles will be reversed. It is too early to pass judgment on the efficacy of these and other strategies. The division of courses into loosely related 'blocks', for instance, might well disturb the insecure student who wants well-integrated materials. But it might well appeal to the kind of student who wants to think for himself. The limiting case would occur if every course team author decided to 'do his own thing' in polite disregard of the contributions of his colleagues. We would then have the sort of teaching that goes on in almost every conventional university.

Chapter 25

The making of D100 :
A view from the social science Faculty

Michael Drake

First Dean of the Social Science Faculty and Chairman of the
'Understanding Society' *course team*

It could, I suppose, be the prototype of a plane, or perhaps a rocket, or an ocean liner or maybe even a secret agent. In fact, D100 is the code name, recognized by computer and student alike, of the Open University Foundation Course in the social sciences. D for Drake: a little touch of vanity in a digital jungle. (Naturally, arts, science and mathematics took A, S, and M respectively.)

The making of D100 began with the appointment of a ten-man team: two from each of the five disciplines of economics, geography, sociology, psychology and politics. (Geography was moved from arts to social sciences at the last minute.) About 250 people applied for the ten posts. As a group they were not very different from applicants to other universities. Producing a short list was done on the age-old criteria—jobs in institutions one recognized; articles in journals one had heard of; referees whose opinions one respected. The only moderately novel feature in the selection procedure was that each candidate called for interview, was asked to set down his views on how best to produce an inter-disciplinary Foundation Course in the social sciences. The results of all this activity were hardly startling. Of the ten appointed, six had degrees from Oxbridge, two from London. All but one had taught university degree students before: eight in universities, one in a polytechnic. There was plenty of 'solid scholarship' among the publications and experience, like teaching or researching in Australia, West and East Africa, Latin America and the United States. Ages ranged from twenty-three to fifty-four.

Such was the academic core of the team that within two years produced D100. But, of course, D100 itself bears the marks of a far larger number of people—BBC radio and television producers, educational technologists, designers, printers, editors and, what turns it from a mass of print and an image on a screen into a piece of teaching, the 750 part-time tutors scattered throughout the country and marshalled by the fifteen staff tutors (the university's regional academic staff) in social sciences. How all these different people interacted determined the character of the course. The course team chairman's main role was to see that the interaction was reasonably fruitful. This was not always easy. There were four main sources of conflict.

First there were relations among the academics themselves. Like most university teachers, they had been accustomed to operating in their own little private worlds of the classroom and the study. Now they were to be exposed—their writing spurned, their TV and radio performances mocked. They were derided for being old-fashioned or condemned for being too radical. In one form or another this happened to every member of the team. Once the course outline had been decided upon, the team broke up into eight working groups, each responsible for about a month of the students' work. It was interesting to see these groups in operation. The most difficult, and the least successful, were those tackling overtly inter-disciplinary themes. Those presenting mostly single-disciplinary material in a relatively traditional format were the least contentious. Despite the trauma, only one member of the team did not manage to accommodate himself to the demands made upon him by the team as a whole.

Relations between the academic members of the course team and the BBC producers were very variable. Here problems developed largely because of the inexperience of both academics and producers. One or two members of the team had had considerable experience of both television and radio, but the majority had had little or none. On the BBC side, though the senior producer was very experienced, most of his team of production assistants were raw recruits. There was, as one might have predicted, a certain jockeying for power. One incident involved a shirt. It came at the end of a long day in the television studio. Just before the recording was to be made the producer decided that the academic presenting the programme would have to change his shirt: it was too dark. This came after a series of minor bust-ups. The academic refused. The producer then said OK, that's it, no programme. The academic appealed to his academic colleagues (who backed him): the producer got uncompromising support from his people. After ten minutes of eyeball-to-eyeball confrontation, the academic caved in: a technician of appropriate size and with the right coloured shirt undressed. The show went on. A few months later, I saw the same shirt on the same academic worn without comment in another television programme.

Another incident of the early days took place in the BBC bar at the Langham. The argument was over the format of another television programme. I attempted to mediate between a producer and an academic. Tempers rose, drink was spilled, blows were struck. In the end, a compromise was made and one of the best programmes of the entire course emerged, acclaimed by students, staff and the BBC (who exhibited it abroad).

Relations with the printers, designers and publishers also had their ups and downs. One of the decisions made by the course team was to produce a Reader to cover the course as a whole. The decision was made in September 1969. Tenders were submitted by a large number of publishers—they ranged from 70p to £4·20—and the final manuscript had to be delivered by February 1970. Amazingly, all deadlines were met and the threatened penalty payment of £10 per hour, imposed by the printer for late delivery of page proofs, was avoided by herculean efforts at Walton Hall. The tyranny of the deadline is the greatest cross the Open University academic has to bear. Fortunately, during the production of D100 the printing industry in Britain had rather a lot of spare capacity, so that deadlines passed could be accommodated. The printers were very forbearing. Relations with members of the design studio—the photographers, artists and paste-up people—also varied greatly. Some academics with a great interest in this side of the work spent a lot of time in the studio. Others were relatively uninterested and had to be prodded and cajoled into taking any part in the selection of illustrations. Sometimes this led to waste. I remember one artist trying, as he put it, 'to liven up' some economics units by drawing the graphs on top of a collage of coins and notes. Much to his disgust, they did not appear in the final version.

With each of these different groups—academic colleagues on the course team, BBC producers, and the 'print people'—relations were close if not always congenial. But with the part-time teachers and the students they were at best sporadic and often non-existent. The strength of the OU system is that it produces very expensive, high quality, teaching materials which it disseminates very cheaply. But this has not been done without a correspondingly revolutionary shift in the role of the academic. Gone is the medieval craftsman, producing everything on his own premises and meeting his customers face-to-face. Now we have an academic entrepreneur, a co-ordinator of other men's skills, directing a vast army of tutors. The tutors, whatever their personal academic qualifications—and some are very high—are, when working for the Open University, very much an academic proletariat. The success of the system depends upon their sticking closely to the materials devised by the course team. Novel ways of teaching the course, yes; but additions to the materials, lectures on tangential themes, a fundamental questioning of the course structure, no. The task of mediating the course team's wishes to the part-time tutors lies in the hands of the fifteen social science staff tutors who live in the various regions and who recruit and supervise them. The monitoring of essays marked by the part-timers is largely in their hands: the standardization of marking is largely dependent upon them. It is a thankless task. There are some 750 tutors and counsellors working on D100. They are of all ages and backgrounds—some dedicated to what they see as the ideals of the Open University, some merely hard-up. A similar problem of relationships arises with regard to the 200 or so part-time academics who man the D100 summer schools. Again, the course team sets precise objectives. Unless these are followed rigorously, the students will not be taught the course. Yet the academics who staff these schools, coming from the conventional system where every teacher is king in his classroom, may well find the system uncongenial. Not surprisingly the turnover of summer school staff is high.

Finally, there are the students. The course team need never meet the students except at the Summer school, at which every academic is contractually bound to put in a two-week stint. Some find the isolation disturbing; for others, of course, it is blissful. The lack of direct contact is overcome to some extent by an elaborate system of monitoring and reporting and there are many indirect contacts. Students often write or 'phone members of the course team. Inevitably in an institution dealing with such large numbers of students, procedures must be highly bureaucratic and the computer must play a central role. Equally inevitably, some students, tiny in percentage terms but disturbingly high in actual numbers, seem to get across the system. They do not receive their course materials, their tutor is a dud, their summer school allocation form goes astray. Hardly surprisingly some students turn savagely on the academics. A 'sadistic incompetent' was one term levelled at me by an irate student.

The making of D100 involved a large number of people whom the conventional academic would rarely meet, and a host of problems he would never face. As the first course, it was the testing ground. It taught us a great deal. The experience can never be repeated, although D100 Mark Two is due for 1975. It is perhaps a measure of its awesome character that the Faculty of social sciences has found it very difficult to appoint a chairman willing to take on the task of assembling another course team for the remake.

Chapter 26

A view from the science Faculty

Peter J. Smith
Senior Lecturer in Earth Sciences

In January 1971 over 6,000 students embarked upon the Open University's Science Foundation Course, thereby increasing the first-year science population in British universities by almost 50 per cent. The following year this exercise was repeated only slightly more modestly; and in January 1973 several thousand more students followed in the wake of their pioneering predecessors. My point in mentioning these statistics, however, is neither to impress nor to validate the laws of supply and demand, but simply to draw attention to what, on the face of it, is a paradox. For is it not a fact that the sudden expansion in science education represented by the Open University has coincided with a period of exceptionally high unemployment, even among highly trained scientists and technologists? Moreover, has not the belief, so fashionable during the early 1960s, that the Britain of the 1970s would find itself with a dire shortage of scientists, faded into the annals of history? And is there not more than a suspicion in some quarters that what the world needs now is not an acceleration in the pace of scientific advance but a breathing-space in which to rethink the relationship between society and a technology which is, in some sense, out of control?

These are contentious questions; I believe they are of sufficient merit to warrant a justification for the spectacular proportional increase in scientific education which the Open University has chosen to foster. In personal terms, of course, the justification is not in doubt. The proportion of the relevant age-group able to enter the university today—modest though it may be in comparison with, say, the United States—is much higher than it has been over the past thirty years or so; and that being the case, many people must have been deprived of a university education for no other reason than insufficient places being available at the critical time. I would go further than to say that this historic injustice must be remedied by asserting that every citizen, of whatever age, has a right to be educated up to the level of his or her ability. But, however one defines the educational backlog, there are no reasonable grounds for compounding injustice by imposing unnecessary restrictions on the choice of the broad subject area of study. Within reason, personal freedom of choice thus dictates that the Open University offer options in a field of such manifest importance as science.

I make no pretence that this is anything but an idealistic view; nor am I naïve enough to suppose that any government would finance such a vast enterprise on moral grounds alone. The fact is—and I do not object to it in principle—the Open University only proved politically viable because someone, somewhere, was able to define its role in national—as opposed to moral or personal—terms. But if the assumptions upon which this national need was originally based are no longer valid, can the OU still justify its large investment in science today?

This seems to me to be such an obvious question to ask; and yet, surprisingly perhaps, I have never heard anyone pose it. If any eyebrows have been raised at Open University science at all, they have been raised not to ask whether we *should*, as a matter of principle, be teaching science, but whether, in practice, we *can* properly teach science at a distance given its practical nature. How, the argument goes, can Open University science education be viable as long as students are unable to spend long hours in the laboratory acquiring the skills which form the whole basis of the scientific enterprise? The short answer is that there is more than one way of skinning a cat, and that by a judicious combination of home experiments, televised demonstrations involving student activity, and laboratory-based summer schools, the time spent on practical work by our students is at least comparable to that spent by students in a conventional university. Moreover, simply *because* we are subject to the disadvantages of distance we have had to think out rather more clearly than university teachers are normally wont to do just what it is we are trying to achieve with the practical components of our courses. The average university practical class is a dull, apparently purposeless, uninspiring, irrelevant existence more concerned, in the physical sciences at least, with connecting little bits of wire to grey boxes with dials, than with demonstrating the nature of science. This is not to pretend that we have fully solved the problems of practical science either; but we at least feel that we have made a start in redefining objectives.

And it is this question of objectives which brings us right back to the original question of why the Open University is teaching science in the first place. For the doubts, such as those about the viability of science at a distance, seem to be based on an implicit assumption that we are trying to emulate science education in the conventional university; that in offering science education at university standard to people who, through no fault of their own, missed out the first time around, we are seeking to duplicate precisely the sort of training they would have received had conventional university places been available. In my view this is not the case at all.

There is, of course, one way in which the Open University must be comparable with other universities—in its standards. Standards are notoriously difficult to define and ensure; but without wishing to appear in any way complacent, I am convinced that through a combination of our own previous experience in the wider university community (my own was at the University of Liverpool and Imperial College, London) and the use of such devices as the system of external examiners, ou science maintains the standards we have come to expect of all British universities. There is thus no question of introducing a multi-level set of standards such as that which obtains in, for example, American higher education. So what is at issue here is not the question of level but that of content and attitudes; and it is the aims and achievements of ou science in the latter context which diverge from those of the conventional university, and which must be seen against the background of the failure of the conventional university system in general to respond quickly, or at all, to the changing relationship between society and science, or even to maintain its role as an instrument of true education as opposed to purely vocational training.

British university science has long been somewhat ambivalent in its attitude to the outside world. Historically, the great impetus to science education in the nineteenth century came about as a result of Britain's abysmal industrial failure at the Paris exhibition of 1867, a failure which Lyon Playfair put down to the lack of 'industrial education for the masters and managers of factories and workshops'. One consequence was that science came to be advocated for its practical benefits rather than its intellectual content and, as Sir Eric Ashby has pointed out, 'science education tended to be regarded as more suitable for artisans and the lower middle classes than for the governing classes'. Nevertheless, there has always coexisted with this utilitarian view the traditional German concept of knowledge for its own sake; and one could argue that it was the dominance of this ideal of science as a cultural and intellectual force which led directly to the great achievements of British science during the early part of this century.

What upset any balance there might have been in university science was world war II, which demonstrated quite clearly to political leaders that science could be a potent force for the achievement of political ends. The result was vastly increased state support for science, the near-total dependence of universities on government finance, and an implicit assumption from then on that university science departments exist solely to satisfy the needs of the state. Whilst this has had its beneficial aspect in tending to destroy ivory-tower elitism, it has been the politicians who have effectively defined the national need. To politicians, therefore, a university science department is little more than a scientific manpower factory; and the universities have responded by interpreting trained manpower as a set of automatons whose prime function is to be crammed with as many facts as possible in the shortest possible time.

The ironies in this situation are numerous. The body of scientific knowledge is now so large that any attempt to cram a student with all the information he is likely to require in his subsequent work is doomed to failure from the outset. It is an impossible task; and any attempt to undertake it must inevitably result in a failure to equip the student with the basic principles he genuinely needs to be adaptable to any subsequent position in which he may find himself. The second point is that the obsession with vocationally trained manpower has obscured the fact that, as M. C. McCarthy showed some years ago, only about 30 per cent of science graduates are destined for research and development anyway. Two-thirds of science graduates are trained for jobs which do not exist and are thus thrown into the frustrations of having to perform tasks for which their training is ill suited. And third, many of the premises upon which society's needs for large numbers of scientific specialists were based are probably no longer valid.

In my view, the prime function of Open University science (apart from its general contribution in the context of a 'university of the second chance') is no more nor less than to attempt to correct the distortions which conventional university science has perpetrated upon society. Thus in positive terms, I want to see the Open University produce not scientific specialists but generalists (hitherto the victims of intellectual snobbery); not students whose ultimate aim is to join the ranks of the researchers and developers but people who, equipped with a knowledge of the nature, principles and methodologies of science, will go out to be civil servants, politicians, journalists and managers; not automatons to whom science is a mere factual catalogue but people with a rounded view of the cultural and intellectual nature of science; not graduates completely oblivious to the interactions between science and modern society but people capable of making rational decisions about science in a science-based society.

The national need I define is thus more related to the quality of life than to the gods of economic growth although, ironically, I suspect that growth would be far from being the loser in a more scientifically aware society. I would say that the aim is to increase scientific literacy in a country which is, in the scientific sense, disgracefully illiterate. Consequently I am unable to share the misgivings of many of my colleagues at the suggestion that the Open University should concern itself with eighteen-year-olds. To my mind, we are trying to do something which most conventional universities have conspicuously failed to do; and what we are trying to do is applicable to students of any age.

Chapter 27

A view from the mathematics Faculty

G. A. Read

Senior Lecturer in Mathematics

In the mathematics Faculty we discovered to our surprise that it was possible to find members of the Foundation Course team holding almost every conceivable opinion on almost every topic. Such a situation would not surprise a social scientist, but to a mathematician it is devastating. For years we have been trained to deal with clear cut problems for which, even if they cannot be solved, we can be certain that a solution is indeed a solution. How can you apply such training to the assessment of a television programme or to the writing style of one of your colleagues? Add to this the fact that mathematicians are taught to be sceptical of everything, indeed the most powerful weapon in their armoury is the counter-example, and that people appear to be almost as sensitive about their writing style and their television programmes as about their driving ability, and you have a potentially explosive situation.

The decision to make the University 'Open' in the sense that no previous qualifications were required had probably a more profound effect on the mathematics Faculty than any other. It is simply impossible to study the subject at anything but a trivial level without, for example, some knowledge of elementary algebra. Our Foundation Course had to be of 'university standard' and although the Open University had no entrance requirements we clearly had to assume some entry behaviour. Exactly what 'entry behaviour' we were assuming was a topic which arose constantly at our meetings, often from the most unlikely items on the agenda. In order to overcome the problem we commissioned one of our members to write a series of 'refresher booklets' and a diagnostic test which, together with advice from the tutors, would hopefully enable the students to decide if they had the necessary knowledge before starting the course.

Not only do our students have widely varying backgrounds but they also intend to study a wide variety of courses after the mathematics Foundation Course. For some it will lead to a serious study of mathematics, for others, going on to science or technology, the subject is just an addition to their 'tool kit'. For the social science or arts student the course may be their only glimpse of advanced mathematics. It isn't difficult to imagine the prolonged discussion at the course team meetings on the most suitable content and style of such a course, but finally we agreed that the course should range over a wide variety of topics and should concentrate on mathematical ideas rather than simply introduce the student to a set of techniques. I must say that initially these decisions worried me a great deal, but in retrospect I believe that we were right. The choice of notation in the Foundation Course caused me the greatest concern, and I still feel that the emphasis has been placed too heavily on the structural advantages of our 'new' notation at the expense of basic manipulative skills which are more in tune with the 'old' notation. But such decisions must be taken.

With the immense cost of our texts or television programmes it would be very wrong, in my opinion, to allow a single individual to have total control of the production of any specific item. For our isolated students even minor errors can cause a lot of unnecessary trouble, and even the most eminent people are capable of making the most awful blunders. If you make a stupid error on a television programme then it is, of course, very public and possibly very expensive. For reasons of cost a programme may have to be transmitted for several years complete with your foolish mistake. One of us said 'less than' and wrote $>$ (greater than) on a particular programme, and it just would not be economic to remake the programme for such a minor slip. I made a similar mistake on one of my programmes but I seem to be the only person to have noticed it. The arguments over remaking a particular programme rebound between educational desirability on the one hand and cost on the other. Very often we find ourselves in discussions over 'cost-effectiveness', a subject for which a purely academic training might often be a positive handicap.

The television and radio programmes form probably the most difficult area of our work. There are technical problems which are peculiar to the presentation of mathematics. For example, the number of symbols which will fit onto the screen is very limited and the student is unable to refer back to previous work as he would naturally wish to do when following a lecture at a blackboard. We have tried to circumvent these and other problems on a number of programmes by concentrating on the basic mathematical ideas involved, illustrated by models, animated film, industrial application and other techniques. The sceptic will probably regard such devices as unnecessary paraphernalia which are at best an extension of the normal teaching aids, but this is to miss the point. Through the television programmes we are often, so to speak, pouring mathematics in through a different hole in the student's head; and we hope to implant a deep personal appreciation of the mathematical ideas by giving him a strong visual experience to cling to. I can think of many instances where this approach has been highly successful; one example, I will guarantee that every mathematics student associates the Taylor Series with a certain piece of computer film, and a cam-cutting machine with linear interpolation.

Much has been made of the fact that a high proportion of our students are teachers, and consequently, the argument goes, we are not fulfilling the social need to which we owe our existence. But in the long term I find it most heartening that the university seems to have been accepted so totally by our colleagues in other branches of education, particularly the schools. It seems to me that no single thing could improve the social conditions in our country more efficiently than the educational system and for that above all else we need good teachers.

The teachers who do not yet know too much about the university may well be forced to learn. We have heard stories of school children who have watched our mathematics television programmes and have then arrived in the classroom the next day with absolutely unanswerable questions for their teachers. Perhaps we are lucky that they cannot so easily put the questions directly to us.

We do have some facilities for dealing with feedback from the students, but in the main we hope to foresee the difficulties which students will have with the material as we produce it. This is yet another reason for working in a group, but it is also a source of dispute. We have still not adequately resolved the problem even for those courses which have run through a complete year.

Simple surveys among students will certainly reveal the items which are much too difficult, but in the main student opinion is very untrustworthy. If the students say that a television programme is too easy, is it because the content is trivial, or have we taught the subject so well that it just appears easy? Even if certain material is too easy for the majority of students, what of the possibly large minority?

We have at least one opportunity during the year to meet our students face to face, and that is at the summer school. These sessions have been enormously successful from many different points of view. For me it was quite an emotional experience to see the first group of about 300 students, all studying the course which we had worked on for so long. There they all were in the flesh, real live people working like mad to understand the course that we had produced. Some of them had given up their summer vacation to attend the school (which meant that their families gave up their holiday too) and all of them intended to get their money's worth. The amount of work they are prepared to do is astonishing, even to those of us with experience of teaching mature students.

Chapter 28

A view from the technology Faculty

G. S. Holister

First Dean of the Technology Faculty

In 1968 I was occupying a rather uncomfortable chair of engineering mechanics at a large State university in the United States. I had taken up this position when I had moved from a lectureship in civil engineering at the University of Wales, and I had never really settled to the anonymity and lack of administrative authority that go with such a chair in the United States—at least in the large State universities.

A particularly uncreative and unrewarding position was alleviated only by the fact that I had managed to obtain a one day a week appointment as adjunct professor of music in the Faculty of arts and could therefore pursue my favourite hobby, the classic guitar, as part of my academic duties. It had become my habit to read the *Observer* on a Sunday morning in the hope of finding a suitable post back in Britain. So it was that I saw one of the Open University's first advertisements.

It took me several months to extricate myself from my various commitments in the United States, and I eventually arrived at Belgrave Square in May 1969 to find several of the new deans already in post and under way with a full head of steam. The concept of a Keele-type Foundation Course in the various disciplines had already emerged, and as a late-comer I had to make some fairly urgent decisions concerning the role of technology at the Open University and whether there was a need (and room) for a Foundation Course in technology. The two problems were not connected.

I spent a lot of time talking to former academic colleagues and thinking about the type of technology that was appropriate to the modern world and this new and revolutionary institution. My thoughts followed the following lines:

(a) The rate of development in technology had up till quite

recently depended on, first, man's ability to develop and use suitable materials for his needs, and second, his ability to find and control suitable sources of power. Within the last fifty years, however, our progress appeared to be limited not by the availability of materials or sources of power but by our limited understanding of the very complexity of the systems we were developing. Most of the exciting developments in technology (general systems theory, operational research, etc.) seemed to me to be in this area of trying to understand and control complex systems (to me, the triumph of the moon landings was above all else the successful human control of an unbelievably complex technological system). Control (of mechanical and electrical mechanisms) was an established part of an undergraduate curriculum in engineering, but I decided that a modern technology curriculum should include strong elements of systems theory that would take in both engineering control theory and the newly developing disciplines of management science and cybernetics.

(b) Because of the necessarily small size of Faculties in the Open University (four or five disciplines per faculty) it would be quite impossible, even if it were desirable, to split technology into the traditional engineering disciplines (civil, mechanical, electrical, chemical, etc.) I therefore decided upon an engineering mechanics discipline to cover those areas (structures, strength of materials, etc.) that are common to civil and mechanical engineering; a materials discipline to cover those areas usually taught in departments of metallurgy, but to include also modern materials such as plastics, ceramics and composites, and a discipline of electronics design and communication to cover the most relevant areas of electrical engineering, electronics and communications, and to include an interdisciplinary overlap into the area of control theory.

(c) With the above discipline areas pretty well sorted out in my mind, I felt that the creative design ability that is at the heart of most technological developments should be catered for by a separate discipline which, like the systems discipline, should start with the broader concepts initially. Since creative design (as distinct from the more formalized engineering development methodology often taught as engineering design) requires the generation in the student of an ability for synthesis (rather than analysis) this is a particularly challenging area where traditional teaching methods have a doubtful validity.

So there, I persuaded myself, I had a rationale for the five technology disciplines, and at the same time a provisional brief for a Foundation Course that would be highly inter-disciplinary. Both in regard to such a Foundation Course and to the role of the Faculty as a whole, I felt that a concern for and systematic study of the social and environmental aspects of technology was essential. Certainly environmental problems were approachable only by means of systemic and inter-disciplinary methods and I felt convinced that any Faculty of technology that did not concern itself with such problems could not claim to be either modern or responsible, whether socially or academically. (This was 1969 —before the environment had become a fashionable subject.)

With the initial appointments of the five professors (of systems, engineering mechanics, materials, electronic design, and communications and design) we began to study the sort of Foundation Course in technology that, as a group, we wished to create. We decided that the greatest need was for a Foundation Course whose aim was to give an understanding of technology (its aims, techniques, and side-effects) to those students who had no intention of becoming engineers. We considered such students to be at least as important as the committed technology students. Bridging the gap between the two cultures is largely by one-way routes. Scientists and technologists can, if so disposed, cultivate interests in the arts, but an appreciation of the scope, implications and relevance of scientific and technological matters is less readily accessible to the student of the humanities—yet businessmen, trade union leaders, politicians and the citizens of democratic societies must nowadays repeatedly make individual or corporate decisions of a technological nature. Such a course would also serve as an effective broad base from which committed technology students could subsequently launch into their more specialized higher level courses.

In 1972 4,000 students enrolled in T100, 'The Man-Made World', our highly interdisciplinary, case-study-oriented Foundation Course; a second-level half credit course in electronics had been produced in parallel to it, and courses in systems, management science, materials, mechanics, design and environmental studies were planned for presentation in 1973, 1974 and 1975. It is going to take us nearly ten years before we can offer to students a complete á la carte choice of subjects covering all the major areas of technology, and only then will we begin to have a clear idea of the success of our overall plans.

Chapter 29

A view from the educational studies Faculty

Phillip Williams

Professor, Educational Studies

The challenge

Most British universities offer a variety of courses of study in education. Some universities include the study of education as part of their offerings for first degrees; the postgraduate certificate meets the needs of the newly qualified graduate who wishes to teach; the B.Ed. fulfils the requirements of the rising standards in colleges of education; the M.Ed. fosters the academic standards of experienced educators; advanced diplomas in education set standards of entry to M.Ed. courses for experienced non-graduate applicants; there are many specialist diplomas catering for the needs of experienced teachers with specific interests and backgrounds.

These courses largely evolved in response to the needs of the educational system and few would want to deny that the teachers of education in British universities have worked hard to meet new demands. Equally, few would claim that the resulting pattern of education courses is ideal on grounds of content or of coherence. The 1972 James Report on Teacher Education and Training is one signal of this concern. Hence the Faculty has been offered the chance to design from scratch a set of education courses from under-graduate to Ph.D. level at a time of major national interest in the teaching of education.

The problems

The Planning Committee correctly predicted that a high proportion of the students of the Open University would be teachers wishing to obtain a graduate qualification, and that a high proportion of these teachers would want to read educational studies.

The implication of this situation for educational studies lies in the range of courses which a large student body is likely to demand and which the Faculty and university should have an obligation to meet.

A second problem relates to practical work. This is not quite the same as the problems faced by science-based Faculties. In educational studies the laboratory is primarily the classroom. How can thousands of prospective students, mirroring the national distribution of all Open University students, be given access to classrooms and, more importantly, be adequately supervised?

Yet another problem relates to the range of skills which students bring to the courses in educational studies. An educational studies course can be taken by an experienced teacher with a recent college of education qualification; but the same course can also be taken by someone who has had no experience of education at all.

Should the purpose of our courses be to build on the educational experience of the great majority of students, so enhancing their understanding of the teaching situation and of the education system? Or should we produce courses which teach the fundamental concepts of educational studies in such a way that the minority of non-teachers are as little disadvantaged by their lack of educational background as possible?

The wide range of previous experience of students also poses problems for the university's academic structure. Should the award of a degree be granted after the normal number of credit exemptions, i.e. one exemption for each year of approved higher education experience up to a maximum of two credit exemptions? This is, with some minor exceptions, the rubric which the Open University has normally adopted.

But if this were to be applied to education students, then the interesting situation would arise whereby many ex-college of education students could convert their teaching certificates into B.Eds after one year of full-time study at a number of British universities; but in order to convert to an Open University degree, they would be required to gain four of the six credits the university requires. On our normal conversion ratio, four credits implies the equivalent of no less than two years of full-time study.

The response

First let us consider how these problems shaped the Faculty's response.

Postgraduate courses, specialist diplomas and research activities had necessarily to take second place to ensuring that those students who wished to gain a degree in educational studies as soon as possible could do so. This implied providing at least the minimum number of educational studies courses at undergraduate level, and, hopefully, a sufficient number of courses to allow some choice. Paradoxically, it is now, in the early years of the university, that pressure for courses is likely to be at its highest: and it is now that the choice offered is at its most restricted.

The questions surrounding practical work led quickly to a decision that certainly for the time being there would be no attempt to award a Certificate of Education, thus avoiding the problems of organizing teaching practice. But deciding to concentrate on educational studies without the professional bonus of a Certificate of Education does not mean that practical work can be ruled out altogether. For example, courses which involve a study of child development necessitate work with children. So one of the first courses launched included several practical exercises, one of which involved seeking the co-operation of every Local Education Authority in the country so that facilities for the work could be made available. This experience and some survey results lead to three conclusions. First, that most but not all Education Authorities are willing to allow this sort of exercise to proceed. Second, that organizing it involves a considerable amount of work on the part of the university's regional services and others. Third, that most students gain enormously from the exercise and appreciate the importance of practical work.

The minority of non-teachers in the educational studies courses did not rise about 10 per cent in any of the first courses the Faculty established. Since the courses have, to some degree been aimed at improving the skills and knowledge of the educator, it is almost inevitable that the 90 per cent or more of students with recent direct experience of the classroom might be at an advantage. But the comments which have so far come in from our tutors do not suggest that the non-teacher minority of students are in any sense markedly disadvantaged.

The problem of exemptions has been dealt with by a compromise. Teachers with three years of full-time higher education in a college of education can be allowed to claim three exemptions, and not two, provided the courses which they take at the Open University are, in majority, educational studies courses.

The three areas in which the Faculty elected to start teaching focused on the implications for education of a study of the child, of society and of the curriculum respectively. Thus the 'Personality Growth and Learning' course team attempted to use the interaction between personality and learning as a theme linking the topics in educational psychology which that course presented. The 'School and Society' course team presented its area of study from the standpoint of symbolic interactionism rather than the more conventional structural sociology approach. The 'Curriculum' team, too, developed a course which differed from orthodox curriculum courses.

Another principle which guided the choice of courses was the range of their appeal. Thus it would have been interesting and quite logical to have started the child-centred courses with a course geared to the development of very young children. But it seemed more appropriate to offer a course which appealed to a wider range of students, irrespective of the age-range with which they are mainly acquainted. Similarly, it would have been of interest and of national importance to offer a course aimed at helping teachers of secondary school mathematics improve their skills. But it was decided that as a first offering in this field the Faculty would put on a course which was concerned with the curriculum in general.

These first three courses were designed as second level courses, available to anyone with a credit in a Foundation course. Two new half-credit courses, first presented in 1973, build on some of the concepts taught in these courses and are, therefore, designated as third-level courses. 'Methods of Educational Enquiry' is intended to improve the appreciation of educational research and develops some of the skills which 'Personality Growth and Learning' taught. 'Education, Economy and Politics' examines current issues in the field described by its title and builds on some of the ideas discussed in 'School and Society'. Another second-level half-credit course, 'Language and Learning', is an interdisciplinary course within the Faculty, integrating philosophical, psychological and sociological contributions to the study of language.

Although the Faculty's effort has been principally directed to the preparation of undergraduate courses, one post-experience course has been mounted; it deals with developing competence in teaching reading, a subject of considerable national concern, and is aimed particularly at the teaching of middle-order reading skills. One of the original intentions of the Faculty was to make a contribution to the preparation of educational administrators. The first course in this area will be offered at second level in 1974. In the same year the Faculty will also offer a course on urban education, the first of a number of 'problem-centred' courses, in which some of the skills acquired in earlier courses will be applied to educational issues.

There are, of course, several areas in which additional offerings are needed, for example, in the philosophy of education, the history of education, or comparative education. These are all possible areas for future growth.

Already a scheme of collaboration between the University and Milton Keynes College of Education is being organized, in which students at the College will take some of the university's courses. This development, while of interest to the whole university, is of particular concern to this Faculty. It indicates another role which the Faculty may be called upon increasingly to play—that of an agent for the preparation of courses to serve the needs of other institutions concerned with higher education in the post-James era.

Chapter 30

A view from the arts Faculty

Arthur Marwick

Professor of History

In the earliest plans for the Open University a tremendous emphasis was placed on the notion of the integrated approach to academic study.

In the first two years of course production, the arts Faculty perhaps tried harder than any other Faculty to maintain the essentials of the original approach. Arguably, however, the intended integrated approach, from the start, broke down into a multi-disciplinary approach. Devising the broad outlines of the initial Foundation Course took up months of argument and discussion during the spring, summer and autumn of 1969 among the dozen or so academics then in post. Sometimes full of impetuous enthusiasm, sometimes scared out of our wits, we advanced upon, then cautiously withdrew from, the title which had somehow taken vague shape: 'Civilization and Culture'. This fearsome title, as it now seems to me, gives an idea of where the thrust of the course was clearly thought to be; but in the end we settled for the plain, if still ambiguous, 'Humanities: A Foundation Course'. Some of us, guided by our educational technologist, put great stress on the idea of clearly enunciated aims and objectives; others found this exercise potentially stultifying. Eventually aims were settled upon, but it cannot really be said that these aims are given great or consistent prominence throughout the course.

On the other hand, in a curious way, it seems that something with a genuine coherence of its own did emerge. Many of us felt that within the course there should be elements of foundation study in the basic principles and methods of the individual arts disciplines. Thus the first substantial section of the course takes the form of separate introductions to history, to literature, to history of art, and to music; a separate introduction to logic was devised to run concurrently throughout the course, and philosophy was to introduce itself later on in the form of a study of Descartes. This first section of the course ends with an attempt to bring literature, music and art history together in an integrated study. The next section of the course, which in a sense gives it its characteristic mad, but not unmethodical, flavour, consists of a series of case studies: Socrates, *The Gospel of Mark*, Vasari's *Lives of the Artists*, Shakespeare's *Hamlet*, Descartes, and Mendelssohn's rediscovery of Bach's *Saint Matthew Passion*. Originally it was thought that these case-studies would reveal how different disciplines could be brought to bear on one particular subject for study. In the upshot they became very largely (though not exclusively) single-disciplinary exercises. Anything approaching real integration has only been achieved in the final section of the course: a study of the cultural implications of the industrialization process. By any standard this part of the course is an outstanding success (I had no direct part myself in writing it). The course does, I believe, have a real accumulative unity, proceeding from methodological studies of the separate disciplines, through case studies which allow for a minor element of cross-disciplinary work, to a genuine integrated conclusion. When, after a further year, the time comes for revision, my own purely personal view would be that all we need to do is to place more explicit stress upon the links between the several elements of the course.

There can be no doubt that working closely with academics in other disciplines is an enormously rewarding experience, which up to a point helps to compensate for the lack of substantial contact with students and for the rather limited contact one tends to have with other academics in one's own subject. While we all accepted that our second-level courses should also be multidisciplinary, if not really integrated, I think most of us did look forward with some enthusiasm to the opportunity of preparing single-discipline courses in our own special subjects at later levels. The second-level courses have, I think, turned out to be rather strikingly successful. The period concept on which they are based is very much that of the Dean, Professor Ferguson, though it is one that, as a historian, I naturally find peculiarly acceptable. Something of the case-study approach has been retained in both the 'Renaissance and Reformation' and 'The Age of Revolutions', but on the whole the fairly firmly delimited historical frame has provided the opportunity for a more extended move towards integration. Curiously, several senior academics now turning out the first of the specialist courses have expressed regret for the good old days of working together on the multi-disciplinary courses, and have suggested that in future plans we might again turn seriously towards this kind of work.

In the Foundation Course in arts, academics from outside the Open University were used quite extensively in radio and television programmes, but not at all in the written correspondence material. In second-level work, where slightly more use was made of outside academics, it became strongly apparent that it is very difficult for someone outside the system to adapt quickly to the writing of structured OU correspondence material. However, the two second-level courses have presented a galaxy of talent in the television and radio broadcasts. Our students see and hear a range of distinguished authorities which it would be beyond the resources of any single university in the country to offer to their own students.

For most of us, television and radio work was one of the perks of the job to which we most looked forward. Comment on academic performance in front of the cameras has been mildly unfavourable: there is an unresponsiveness about the camera, when compared with the exuberant pleasure of bouncing off a live audience, that tends to produce a mannered stiffness. Yet one or two programmes have achieved a success well outside the confines of Open University teaching: John Dankworth's *Instruments of the Orchestra*, made for Gerald Hendrie's music units, bids fair to become the classic short film on its subject; Godfrey Vesey's radio programme on 'The Princess and the Philosopher' was entered for the Japan prize; and Graham Martin's 'D. H. Lawrence's Eastwood' has been much praised. Perhaps the greatest immediate success has been achieved by programmes which have departed least from conventional broadcasting wisdom. The real challenge is to try to do something new, and to make it come off. Making a programme which genuinely fits into the structure of a course is hard work: personally, I operate on the formula that one 25-minute TV programme involves an input of 100 hours of academic work. And the creative, managerial, and executive burden on individual producers is of course immense.

The burden of academic work, however, falls in the direction of writing correspondence units. At times the seemingly endless process of planning, writing, revising, discussing, revising again, and again, seems like a steady decline into the land of madness and despair; at other times it offers all the joys of facing up to totally new intellectual and logistic problems and coming up with solutions. In general, the arts Faculty has opted for the 'tutorial in print'. That is to say, we have tried to recreate a tutorial or seminar situation in our written units, from time to time prodding students with the same sort of questions that we would ask in the tutorial situation, then following this up with the sort of answers that might be given and a discussion of them.

Third-level arts courses now in operation include 'The Nineteenth-Century Novel and its Legacy', 'Problems of Philosophy' and 'War and Society'. Inevitably the content of these courses reflect the specialist interests of, respectively, the Professor of Literature, the Professor of Philosophy and the Professor of History. In 1974 these three courses will be joined by 'The Development of Instruments and their Music', and in 1975 by 'History of Architecture and Design, 1890–1939'. I for one cannot withhold my admiration for the sense of commitment and faith of those of my colleagues who are announcing now courses to be *written* over a span of three, four, or even five years (I say written, not planned: I think certain sectors of the university have been much too reluctant to plan in advance, so that the final shape of an Open University honours degree still remains pretty nebulous). There should be a fourth-level history course, involving a private research project, in 1974, and an interesting, though necessarily limited range of other courses at all levels will be available in 1974 and 1975 (including a second-level half-course on 'The Early Roman Empire and the Rise of Christianity'). It is, I think, very much to the credit of the Faculty that it has taken a lead in sponsoring the teaching of history of science— 'Science and the Rise of Technology Since 1800' (available 1973) will be followed in 1974 by 'Science and Belief'. Religion should also develop as one of the Faculty's major specialist fields.

The Open University situation has provided a unique opportunity to develop one particular interest of mine in connection with the 'War and Society' course: this is the question of the utility to the historian of archive film material as a primary source. The sixteen television programmes for this course (one a fortnight) are entirely devoted to the presentation of archive film compilations. Because of this, the Open University was able to take a leading part, in co-operation with the British Universities Film Council and the Imperial War Museum, in planning the conference on 'Archive Film in the Study and Teaching of Twentieth Century History', held at the Imperial War Museum in 1972. But, in general, such is the pressure of work, the special pleasures of research and publication outside the university are denied to us: sometimes one would gladly forsake the treadmill to return to the rat race.

The academic is torn between the pleasure of seeing his own name in print, and the pain of reading, and knowing that others are reading, what he has written. The arts Faculty has very deliberately adopted a policy of attributing individual units to particular authors. I fancy that among my own immediate colleagues the worst fears have been stilled for the time being by the favourable reception which course materials have received from those qualified to pronounce upon them.

But the biggest shock comes when, having written one's quota of words for the day, had one's fill of planning meetings for the week, taken daring decisions in respect of courses past, present, and future, when, mentally and physically exhausted, yet with mind already running on to plans for the morrow, one virtuously attends a study centre, to be asked by a student: 'Apart from working part-time for the Open University, what is your *real* job?'

Part VI
The media

Chapter 31

The OU publishing operation

Hamish MacGibbon

Director, Heinemann Educational Books

My wife is an OU student and my job is publishing school and university books. So I have a personal and a professional interest in the OU material—whether it be printed, television, or sound. With two years as a vicarious OU student behind me, I am convinced that the OU course books have opened up not merely a new and fruitful approach to student book design; they have defined the place of the printed page as a teaching aid in relation to other media.

The impact of the course books is immediate: they contain pictures, colour and unusual layout, novel features for most undergraduate texts. The generous use of pictures, even to the extent that they are not always essential to the text, is notable if only as an indication that visual media, television and colour magazines are now accepted as fairly respectable purveyors of serious ideas—a development which is surely being accelerated by the OU. More important than the pictures, however, are the layout and typography, the application of magazine design techniques to achieve a highly specific and sophisticated educational objective. These are not textbooks, but teaching aids which serve as a substitute for lectures, seminar, reading guide and notebook, providing a course in themselves, many of them quite independently of the television and radio programme.

A striking feature of the publications is the unique 'factory' method by which the books are written, designed and printed. Ordinarily, writing, publishing and printing are carried out by at least three separate, economically and geographically independent units: the author, the publisher and the printer. In marked contrast, the OU author, publisher, and even to some extent the printer, are literally under the same roof. One can actually stroll along a corridor from the faculties where the material is being written, to the art studios where the illustrations are being drawn, to the sub-editorial offices, to the extensive typesetting, printing and binding departments, and finally to the dispatch department. The analogy with magazine publication, manifest in the appearance of the books, is here driven home even more forcibly.

This homogeneous writing/publishing/printing function is important in order to achieve the particular blend of content and design which enable the books to perform their multifarious purposes. The dialogue between the faculty members and the designers not only enables the designers to convey the message clearly and faithfully, it also helps the academics to clarify their ideas. But in any case, what makes the team method an absolute necessity is the astonishing volume and speed at which the student material is produced.

Only a handful of academic publishers publish more than two hundred student books a year. The average publication time from receipt of the typescript to the book's appearance on the bookstalls is nine months to a year.

Even in 1971, with only four Foundation Courses, one hundred course books had to be published, not to mention a great many handbooks, brochures and booklets. The schedule for each course unit is sixteen weeks from the completion of typescript to the receipt of bound copies.

Is there a lesson here for commercial publishers? I don't think so. For the ordinary publisher each book is a separate risk proposition to be edited and designed from first principles to suit its particular market, and with an author who usually has to fit proof-correction into his spare time. In terms of speed and volume of production the ou has two supreme advantages: its books are designed within a uniform format and their market is known. This means that machine-space can be booked and every part of the process standardized. Yet again it is more akin to journals than books.

Whatever else it is, the ou is a big publishing business. In 1971 alone the university produced about 4½ million course units; many, but not all, of these were bound as separate soft cover books. The Supplementary Material booklets (which contain broadcast notes, computer-marked assignments, offprint articles, etc.) are also often quite substantial in size; if one includes these, then the total number of bound books and supplementary booklets produced in 1971 was in excess of 4½ million. This is a massive output and makes the ou one of the largest educational publishers in Britain.

Who are the people in this unique publishing organization, and how does it work? It's a good question because the present set-up is far larger and quite different from that originally envisaged as late as mid-1970, only a few months before the first courses began. The fact that it works so well at present is a tribute less, I think, to good management than to the energy, enthusiasm and tolerance of its members.

The process starts, naturally, with the course-writing teams, members of the faculties. While they are writing each course book they simultaneously discuss illustration and special layout problems with the Media Division, who prepare illustrations and, where necessary, take photographs, either in the studio or on location. For pictures from other sources, the writers go to the library staff who obtain the originals and clear copyright. Where the books are to include copyright text material the Publishing Division will arrange terms with the owners. Sixteen weeks before the bound copy delivery date the finished typescript goes to the Publishing Division.

The Publishing Division is responsible for sub-editing—with a staff of over twenty editors—clearing copyright for the course books, and, negotiating terms for Readers and Set Books (240 of them to date and a massive administrative job)—essential course reading published by outside publishers. After sub-editing, each course book goes to the Media Division for layout and integration with the illustrations.

The Media Division is an impressive sight. It includes a large art studio, housing about thirty artists and designers, a photographic studio, and a complete printing works comprising the most up-to-date film-setting, lithographic platemaking, printing and binding equipment. It is the nearest I have seen to a total book production unit. Like the Publishing Division, Media seems to have been formed at the last moment, almost as an afterthought, only months before the first printed material was due to arrive with the students. The head of the division is Douglas Clark. Significantly his training and experience was not in book publishing but in teaching design, printing, magazine and television. He was about to become Head of the Department of Graphic Design at a distinguished college of art when, in 1970, he was offered his present appointment. It has given him a unique opportunity to apply his unusual combination of expertise in graphic communication. Untrammelled by the constraints of traditional book publishing, he has been able to bring a fresh approach to bear on the new design problems presented by the course books. Each book is in the hands of one designer who works in close conjunction with the writers to communicate their ideas accurately without suppressing their own individual styles. In sharp contrast to the usual division of labour between 'creative', illustrators, designers and draughtsmen Clark has a William-Morris-like belief that his designers should be all round artist-craftsmen, and that good mathematical diagrams deserve as much creative effort as impressionistic illustrations.

The week in Media is followed by two weeks at the printers for galleys (first proofs), a week for proof-checking in Publishing, back to Media for paste-up, another week at the printer for book proofs; two more weeks for a final proof-check and then four weeks for the printer to produce bound copies; that leaves three weeks for Correspondence Services to get the book into the hands of each student. Described in one sentence it looks easy—but for anyone in publishing, enough said. Surveying the whole process is Project Control whose daunting job it is to keep every item on schedule—and, besides the course books, that includes numerous records, cassettes and support booklets. To complete the publishing picture there is the Marketing Division; the ou material has immense sales potential to educational institutions not only in Britain, but throughout the world.

ou publishing, and particularly ou print design, has established that the printed page has a central role in mixed-media education. It is a truism that the printed word is no longer the undisputed medium for the mass communication of ideas. All the same, the swing towards non-book media in education has been surprisingly slow. The key factor from the publisher's point of view is that we are now beginning to appreciate the peculiar advantages of print as an adjunct, if not a substitute, for film and sound, if it is used imaginatively, as it is by the ou. From my view of just one ou student's progress I would guess that, had the course books been less comprehensive, and had they been dull to look at, the drop-out rate would have been significantly higher.

The need for a full-scale publishing and design organization to produce printed material seems to have become generally apparent only a few months before the first books were due to reach the students—quite remarkable, given the vast publishing operation I have just described. The long-term significance of the OU as a publishing venture is that it has devised the first workable multimedia teaching approach on a large scale; and the printed page has gained a great deal from the experience. By being juxtaposed to television it has had to reflect television's visual appeal and incorporate some of its style.

Non-book media have so much to offer education that they will inevitably become commonplace in every school and university in the near future. But the OU has shown that print will always be integral if it is adapted and improved to work with, not in competition with, other methods of communication.

Chapter 32

Broadcasting and multi-media teaching

Anthony Bates

Lecturer in Media Research Methods, Institute of Educational Technology

Does the Open University really need broadcasting? And, if so, is it used effectively? It still seems premature to answer either of these questions. Certainly, the research for which I am responsible has not advanced sufficiently to *prove* the validity of my answers. Nevertheless, I am able to look at the use of broadcasting in all faculties from a fairly neutral point of view, since I am not attached or committed to any particular subject area. Also, since my background is not primarily in broadcasting but mainly in educational research and teaching, I am not committed *a priori* to the need for broadcasting. So although what follows is a personal opinion, it is one that stems from an unusual, if not privileged, position in the university.

My answer to the first question is 'yes'. One major justification is an economic one. We are frequently asked: would it not be cheaper to use other methods, such as cassettes, film-loops, or records, instead of broadcasts? Certainly the technology in this area is developing very rapidly. But at present, broadcasting is by far the cheapest way of 'delivering' audio visual materials to o u students.

The financial case for broadcasting

Broadcasting accounts for about 22 per cent of total o u costs, but transmission costs account for only 5–6 per cent of total broadcasting costs. Between 75–80 per cent of this figure is in fact accounted for by *overheads*—equipment, salaries, management, etc. *Production* costs (film, graphics, processing) account for the remaining 15–18 per cent. Any other system of distribution (film-loops, audio-cassettes, video-cassettes, floppy discs, records) would still incur overhead and production costs nearly as high as those of broadcasting. On the other hand, for most non-broadcast material other than print, *distribution* costs are extremely high, because of the materials, postage and processing involved (for instance, a 25-minute 8 mm film-loop cassette, with optical sound-track, costs £12 per copy, excluding production costs and overheads). The quality of the image or sound of non-broadcast material is usually inferior to that of broadcasts. Furthermore, the University receives a massive hidden subsidy for broadcasts in that students are expected to provide their own play-back equipment, namely, television and radio sets. The only other *playback* equipment that is sufficiently widespread in private ownership are record-players, which are available to about 80 per cent of our students, and the university already issues 'floppy discs' for one course, 'Urban Development'; but this is an *addition* to broadcasting. Radio is easily the cheapest medium, averaging about 15p to 20p per student per programme.

The only other system of distribution which at present comes within reasonable limits of cost is the audio-cassette. A transistorized audio-cassette machine, as issued to technology Foundation Course students, both records and plays back and costs £12 per machine (the cassettes cost 40p each). This cost is borne by the university, spread over four years. Any other system of direct distribution at present available, even including lending or hiring equipment to students, becomes prohibitively expensive, although we are experimenting to try to find some cheap film mechanism which can be worked in synchronization with sound tapes.

An alternative to open-network broadcasting may appear to be to provide audiovisual material, not directly to every student, but through the study centres. Even on a Foundation Course, however, with say 6,000 students and 250 available study centres, many students are unable regularly to get to study centres. As the university increases its range and level of courses, the number of students per course sharply decreases. Consequently even if every student could attend a study centre, the costs per student of materials, in the form of cassettes or film-loops, becomes very high, while production and playback costs would remain almost as high as broadcasting costs. So, surprisingly, broadcasting becomes even *more* economical—in comparison with other methods of distribution—as student numbers per course decrease. Broadcasting has the further advantage of allowing the university to keep to one of the basic principles underlying its foundation—enabling students isolated by distance, physical disability or social conditions to study at a university level, without necessarily having to attend regularly any educational institution.

The educational case for broadcasting

Do university-level students *require* audiovisual materials? This is a more difficult case to argue, because educational needs are less easy to define and measure than economic and administrative factors. (Do conventional university students need lectures?)

The strongest argument is that broadcasting provides experiences which are at the moment impossible for our students to achieve in any other way, and that without these experiences the student would not be recognized by other institutions or other universities as having reached a 'degree' standard. At once one can see that this raises some fundamental questions about the whole philosophy of higher education. Is there a minimum set of experiences which need to be acquired before someone can be said to be of degree standard? We certainly know that professional bodies in science and technology are carefully watching both the content and method of our teaching. Consequently scientists and technologists within the Open University are convinced that it is essential to use television for bringing to students experience of experimental situations, if o∪ science and technology courses are to have academic validity in the outside world.

The educational need for broadcasting for courses in other areas, such as humanities, social sciences and mathematics, is perhaps less obvious, but I feel just as valid. Basically, the argument is that broadcasting can more than compensate for some of the features found in a conventional university, but which are less readily available to o∪ students. It is unrealistic to expect the university to provide all the features of a conventional university education.

But the Open University has a different target population: working adults. These have different educational needs from eighteen-year-old school-leavers. Broadcasting can help the Open University achieve teaching objectives which would be impossible or extremely difficult in a conventional university, objectives which are often much closer to the needs of working adults.

For instance, television may be particularly powerful for challenging stereotyped attitudes of adults. It can present a different view of the world, one that is uncomfortable or disconcerting, and which has more impact and conviction than reading or lectures alone. There is some evidence that this is a particularly important function in providing higher education for adults.

Broadcasting can bring to the adult student 'primary source material', which would not be available even to conventional students. By making use of BBC archive material, by special filming and careful editing, aspects of the world can be brought directly to the student, either to illustrate or give concrete examples of the academic principles being taught in the units, or more importantly, to provide students with material to which they themselves can apply what they have learned. In this way, broadcasting forces both the student *and* the teacher to analyse the relevance and power of the concepts being taught. Television and radio also give students access to eminent people and experts, who would find it impossible to write contributions to OU courses because of the time involved, but who can normally find time for a short and often frank and revealing radio or television interview.

Broadcasting is also essential to break down the isolation of the student. Many students never attend tutorials, and even those who do spend more than 90 per cent of their studying time at home. Feedback from students indicates that many of them value the opportunity to see and hear their professors, and that seeing them—often nervous and awkward—before the television camera makes more human and personal what would otherwise be a very remote and impersonal teaching situation. But the broadcasts must also have relevance, must increase understanding of the concepts in the course. For instance, there is a strong feeling in the mathematics faculty that without the support given by television the dropout rate would be much higher. The assumption is that the television programmes assist the students' understanding and lead to quicker assimilation of the material, and, *at the same time*, give students the psychological boost of feeling that they belong to an organization with real people, however remote or distant these may be physically. Students seem to identify strongly with certain of the academic presenters.

To reap the economic benefits of dealing with large numbers of students working at home, Open University teaching must be highly centralized. To allow student assessment under such conditions to be meaningful, and to allow for efficient communication with students at a distance, the teaching must also be carefully planned and worked out well in advance of its dissemination. As it happens, availability to large numbers, centralization of production and extensive pre-planning are also all basic requirements of open network broadcasting. Therefore the two systems are mutually compatible. It is difficult to think of any other educational institution which can meet the basic requirements needed to exploit fully the advantages of open-network broadcasting.

Although the BBC have offered the University thirty hours a week of both TV and radio transmission time, much of this is at times which are either impossible (because students are not at home) or very inconvenient (after midnight or before 6.30 in the morning). Not until 6.00 p.m. on weekday evenings, or during the weekend, are at least 80 per cent of our students at home from work. At the time of writing fifteen of the thirty hours offered by the BBC for both television and radio fell within these times. This gives us for 1973 thirty-six slots per week for television programmes (25 minutes each) and forty-five slots per week for radio programmes (20 minutes each). Since the University is offering the equivalent of twenty-seven full courses in 1973, the ideal situation of providing at least one programme per course per week, repeated once (as on the Foundation Courses) is obviously already unrealistic. Furthermore, twenty-seven full courses is less than half the number planned for the full undergraduate programme.

On the other hand, the amount of air time available for television and radio transmission is strictly limited in Britain. Already the Open University is taking up almost as much transmission time as BBC Schools and Further Education services combined. Even if the Government were to allocate the fourth channel to educational broadcasting, this not only would take some years to implement, but would still be unlikely to meet all the university's needs for broadcasting. The only system which could meet demands of this kind entirely through broadcasting would be cable television, unless ownership of video-cassette recorders becomes as extensive as ownership of television sets is today. It is obvious that for at least into the 1980s, the university is going to be under severe difficulties in providing sufficient means for distributing audio-visual materials to students. Not only is it going to need as much broadcasting as it can get, it is also going to need other more expensive means of distribution, such as audiovision, records, cheap film-loops and systems for playback. These will be needed, not to replace broadcasting, but to complement it.

Since broadcasting is such a scarce resource, have we been using it effectively? My answer to this question is 'no'. There are clear signs that in terms both of student learning and interest, broadcasting has fallen short of many people's expectations. Partly this stems from a general lack of experience in the *design* of a truly integrated multi-media teaching system. Another reason is the lack of knowledge or consideration of the *psychology* of adult learners in a multi-media teaching system. A third reason stems from organizational or *operational constraints*, such as the inability of some students to watch or listen to programmes, which in turn has led to excessive restrictions on the potential use of broadcasting. We knew at the outset that to make sense of the various resources available to us, we would need an integrated approach to the media.

In the Foundation Courses academics often had to write extensive and detailed drafts of correspondence texts before they were able to specify precisely what they wanted to teach. Only then was it possible to decide on the contents of the television or radio programme. This meant that the major conceptual ideas were contained in the correspondence text, and the television and radio programmes merely reinforced or discussed these concepts.

Moreover, pressure on behalf of students in areas where BBC 2 or VHF reception was poor or non-existent led most course teams deliberately to design their courses so that students could, if necessary, manage without the broadcasts. Assessments reflected this policy, being based on the correspondence material. Furthermore, the decision to allocate one television and one radio programme to each Foundation Course unit (one week's work) avoided the necessity for considering any specific instructional policy for broadcasting; each programme would 'grow out' of the relevant correspondence text.

Since 1971, however, there has been a gradual change occurring in the use of broadcasting. Science alone had argued from the beginning that television was essential for its Foundation Course, and had advised students not to take the course if they did not have access to television. 'Science-based' courses (which for some reason included mathematics, as well as technology) were awarded a greater allowance of television programmes per unit at second-level and beyond (a 1:1 ratio, compared with 1:2 for 'arts-based' courses). This arbitrary decision, while causing much dissension in the university, nevertheless has had the effect of forcing 'arts-based' courses to examine much more carefully the function of broadcasting, and in particular how broadcasting fits into the overall design of their courses. The decision also released television from the bondage of having to serve every single unit.

The existence of broadcasting as a unique resource has influenced the choice of objectives for some courses. This can be seen in courses like 'War and Society', where the television programmes are based entirely on archive film material—or in the titles of some of the 1973 or 1974 courses, such as 'The History and Design of Architecture', 'Language and Learning'. To choose objectives for teaching irrespective of the resources available is obviously nonsense. In the Open University the decision to use broadcasting *preceded* decisions regarding the content of most courses. Put another way, the choice of which media we can use is relatively restricted, whereas as a university we have the whole universe of knowledge from which to choose for our content. It makes sense, therefore, to choose both a style and content which maximize our resources.

Some specific functions for broadcasting—such as primary source material, laboratory work, challenging established attitudes—have already been mentioned. Others include the ability of television to demonstrate principles involving two-, three- or even n-dimensional space, to represent, speed up or slow down changes over time, particularly dynamic change involving several functions operating at once, physically to model abstract principles, and to instruct students on how to carry out activities, such as experiments, inverviewing and analysis of material already provided.

Part of my job is to identify and pass on to new course teams those objectives which are particularly appropriate to broadcasting. It is equally important, however, to identify the conditions under which these objectives are likely to be successful, and this means examining the skills of our students in watching, listening to and interpreting broadcasts. One of the reasons why broadcasting has not been as successful as anticipated is that we have paid insufficient attention to the experience, motivation and situation of most of our students.

Their most precious resource is time. There is a tremendous pressure on the students to be instrumental in their approach. If students can achieve good marks for assignments without watching broadcasts, then it is not surprising if students consider broadcasting to be of minor importance.

Second, when programmes break away from the conventional format either of an illustrated lecture or of a highly structured, direct teaching device, without guidance the students will not know how to approach the programme. It is necessary to make clearer to students how they are expected to relate the programme to what they have learned elsewhere in the course. The structure of the programme itself—at least in the early courses—should highlight the main principles embedded in the primary source material. This however, has major implications for course design, in that the programmes and the correspondence material should be developed *at the same time*.

These examples, and some of the justifications for broadcasting, indicate a growing awareness of the need to consider exactly what we need broadcasting for. Some may strike you as post-hoc rationalizations—which indeed they are. Deciding to base part of the Open University's teaching strategy on broadcasting was an act of faith. But, as long as the university can continue to learn, the planners' act of faith will be well vindicated.

Chapter 33

New media in the OU: An international perspective

Richard Hooper

Formerly Senior Producer, BBC Open University Productions

The earliest reference I can find to a 'university of the air' is in an American radio magazine dated May 1922: 'The people's university of the Air will have a greater student body than all our universities put together.'

Full of enthusiasm for this 'new-fangled medium', men were busy prophesying a bright educational future. Here was a miracle machine to carry teaching into every home. Half a century later, radio and television are expanding education in the developed world, as well as in developing countries such as Niger, El Salvador, American Samoa, the Ivory Coast, Thailand and Mexico. The major achievements have been in primary education, with secondary and higher education following more reluctantly behind.

Several years ago, whilst on a Harkness Fellowship studying educational technology in the United States, I came across a few small-scale universities of the air. One had the distinction of working underwater—college credit courses taken at sea via closed-circuit television by the crews of Polaris submarines.

In 1913 Thomas Edison proclaimed the motion picture as the agent of complete school reform. Almost every new product of communications technology has been tried out somewhere, sometime, on education—open-circuit television, fascimile transmission, two-way radio, closed-circuit television, long-distance instruction by computer, talking typewriters, stereovision, radiovision, 16 mm film, 8 mm film, Super 8 mm film, single concept loops, filmstrips, floppy discs, talking books, teaching machines. And everywhere a curious confrontation has occurred —old world with new technology. In a small college deep in the heart of the Oklahoman bible belt I dialled a videotape from a study cubicle in the new $400,000 Learning Center and watched a local nun talk in front of a blackboard for fifty minutes. The tropical airwaves of the tiny Pacific islands of American Samoa carry six channels of educational television in a crash programme of school reform. Television sets are manoeuvred ashore in longboats over coral reefs. When I was there in 1968, the young Samoan children would call out in broken American, 'What is your name? What is your father's name? What is your mother's name?' imitating a language drill just learnt by elder brothers and sisters from their American television teacher.

The United States has pioneered the educational use of television, film and computers. In the 1930s Iowa State University's experimental television station transmitted lecture courses in art, engineering and botany. Louisana State University installed the world's first language laboratory in 1947. In 1955 Pennsylvania State University began its closed-circuit television system backed by Ford Foundation money, and Penn State soon became, for overseas visitors, one of the meccas on the grand tour. A year later, 1956, Ford dollars opened another mecca—Chicago TV College. With its integrated use of television, print, written assignments, trips to museums, lab. sessions, face-to-face and telephone tutorials, Chicago TV College is one forerunner of Britain's Open University.

The Open University's emphasis on correspondence methods of teaching, combined with broadcasting, can be traced to other forerunners—in Japan, Russia and Australia. In Japan correspondence education dates from the nineteenth century. Japan's BBC equivalent, NHK, first linked radio to correspondence education in 1953. By 1970, 156,000 Japanese were taking high school courses via correspondence, broadcasts and weekend schooling, and 134,000 were enrolled in college correspondence courses, backed up by TV and radio broadcasts from NHK.

But the revolutions so often heralded by the media men have not occurred. Many of the closed-circuit systems in American universities had gone into decline when I visited them in the late sixties. Closed-circuit television systems set up along American lines at British universities have been slow to develop. The Midwest Program on Airborne Television Instruction, the world's first educational 'satellite'—a DC6 circling at 23,000 feet above Indiana—has sold off its planes. Computer-assisted instruction projects, following on earlier failures with programmed instruction and teaching machines, have come and gone. American

Samoa's massive use of television has been badly affected by changes of government. In Niger, educational television began as a pilot project in 1964 with twenty-two one-room schools. It is still a pilot project with the original plans to extend the system shelved. Brazil's much publicized project to use a satellite for education has been regularly postponed.

The new media's lack of impact in higher education has many causes. There has been a continuing war between the various new media, with Audiovisual Man fighting Television Man and both fighting Educational Technology Man. This leads at national level to a myriad of competing organizations. In individual universities the television service, audiovisual centre and language labs are all busy practising media apartheid.

Another problem, particularly noticeable in higher education in the USA, has been the status of the media people. The television producer, for example, has tended to be regarded by the academic staff as a technician. He is consulted, if at all, *after* the course content and objectives have been selected by the academic staff. His subject background, again particularly in the USA, has been in low-status academic departments like Speech, Journalism, Education and Television Production.

Perhaps most important of all, the 1950s justification of the use of the new media has in later years been the very cause of their decline. The closed-circuit systems at universities like Pennsylvania State were set up specifically to distribute lectures to more students at less cost. Existing methods of teaching and learning were taken as given. These methods were stretched by use of new technologies—stretched but *not* changed. Many computer-assisted projects have failed because they were only capable of producing drill and practice programmes—the very things that progressive classrooms were trying to move away from.

The Open University was designed to overcome these problems of media fragmentation, media status and media justification. Quantitatively the use of television, radio and computers within the teaching system is small. Even so, the Open University is likely to be regarded as a turning point in the long, often lamentable, history of new media in education.

Media fragmentation has been avoided at the Open University by genuine attempts to carry out an educational technology approach—a systems approach. The idea of the course team, with its tripartite membership of academic staff, BBC producers and educational technologists, has encouraged media coherence. The course team, vested by the university Senate with collective power over the total learning system, is, I believe the OU's single most important contribution to the future of new media in education.

The 'educational partnership' between the BBC and the Open University enables the BBC producer to be involved in content and objectives as well as media and methods. Crucial to making this paper possibility a reality was the BBC's decision to recruit its new production staff from the academic community and train them in broadcasting. A mathematics producer, for example, who has no real fluency in mathematics, would tend to be distrusted by the academics. Such distrust has been a major reason for continuing 'tissue rejection' of new media.

Distrust has been considerably lessened at the Open University by the academic qualifications of production staff, and, by the dual management system. Producers are members of their parent organization—the BBC—but also members of specific university faculties with the relevant committee membership. The same dual management operates with the educational technologists who are members of the Open University's Institute of Educational Technology and also members of teaching faculties. Thus, production staff and educational technologists are not separated off from the academic power structure as they are in most university closed-circuit systems. A more dynamic type of curriculum planning is therefore possible. Under the old system, the media men remain technicians and the media remain cosmetics on the face of education.

This is summed up in the whole notion of 'audiovisual aids'. At Pennsylvania State much the same effect now achieved by closed-circuit television could be achieved by hiring more lecturers. At the Open University, by contrast, the various instructional functions that broadcasting carries out could either not be done at all by other means, or only at unacceptable expense.

If the new media were withdrawn from the university, not only would some of its instructional objectives be affected, but also some of the less tangible objectives that are not strictly 'instructional'. Without the computer, the Open University's mass teaching system would be virtually unmanageable. The mailing of thousands of correspondence texts, the assessment of thousands of students, the need for fast and comprehensive feedback to permit a self-improving system—all require high speed data processing. Open-circuit broadcasting over the BBC national network plays a crucial role in the openness of the institution—as the Vice-Chancellor has said, it is the Open University's 'shop window'. Broadcasting also performs a management function—it paces the student through the correspondence materials, since the programmes related to specific correspondence texts are scheduled in specific weeks. Radio can also act as a fast and cheap fail-safe mechanism, sending out emergency messages. Finally, broadcasting has an important role in building up, to quote the Government White Paper of 1966, 'the corporate feeling of a University'.

But the price of continuing significance for the new media at the Open University is eternal vigilance. In any innovation there is a tendency to move back almost unconsciously to the status quo ante. The Open University does not start from scratch—many of its academic and broadcasting staff are from traditional backgrounds which can so easily reassert themselves. The shortage of good transmission times, allied to the numerical increase in courses, inevitably means a decreasing ratio of broadcast teaching to correspondence teaching. Dissatisfaction with multiple-choice objective testing leads some academic staff to demand the end of all computer-marked assignments. The strongly *verbal* character of any university, allied to the fact that the correspondence text is the crucial medium of learning, threatens to give increasing primacy at the Open University to the written and read word, and lower status to other educational experiences. There is a natural temptation to increase the spoken word—face-to-face tuition—by cutting back on the self-instructional package. In 1972, the second year of teaching, there was a feeling amongst some students that TV and radio were not essential to completing computer-marked and tutor marked assignments and therefore, under pressure of time, could be dropped. But basing assignments on the radio and television components has its problems—not the least of which is the Open University's commitment to students who cannot receive BBC broadcasts and have to rely on cassettes in their study centres.

It is easy to overstate the case of the new media in the Open

University. The shift of title from 'University of the Air' to 'Open University' put the new media in their place, so to speak. Here the new media are not trying to be all things to all men. The importance lies not in broadcasting *per se*, but in its integration with older media of learning and teaching such as print and face-to-face teaching. Where print does the job better, then broadcasting can opt out—and vice versa. This is a crucial change from earlier uses of television, where it was called upon to carry out the revolution singlehanded, to do jobs for which it was not ideally suited. The significance of the Open University is that, structurally, it permits broadcasting to do what it can do, alongside other media doing what they can do.

Perhaps the most important point about the rebaptism from 'University of the Air' to 'Open University' is that it rightly shifts emphasis from means to ends. It is not the use of radio or computers or automated mailing machines that matters. It is their ability to take teaching to where the learner is, rather than compel the learner to come to buildings where teaching is. It is their application to an ideology of open access to a university education, independent of a person's qualifications, independent of where in the nation he or she chooses to live and work. In so many applications of educational technology, media men have preferred to remain preoccupied with their machinery rather than come off the technological fence and make a commitment to broader aims which the machinery might help to bring about.

The Open University has, in a real sense, two ancestries. One is technological. The other is ideological—the notion of a people's university for continuing education throughout life, the notion of deschooling and universities without walls. The significance of the Open University from an international perspective is the way that it has combined on a large scale one ancestry with another.

It is this combination which has now made the open university concept so attractive—and so necessary—to many countries around the world, including those very countries like Japan and the USA which provided early prototypes. The multi-media system devised by the Open University is attractive because it is cost-effective. And the ideology of the Open University is attractive at a time when more and more people are demanding admission to higher education.

A selected bibliography

Official publications

A University of the Air, White Paper Cmnd 2922, HMSO, 1966.
The Open University, Report of the Planning Committee to the
Secretary of State for Education and Science, HMSO, 1969.
The Charter and Statutes of the Open University, The Privy Council,
PC 688, 1969.

General

Bibby, John, 'University expansion and the academic labour market',
Higher Education Review, autumn 1971.
Burgess, Tyrrell, 'The Open University', *New Society*, 27 April 1972.
Donaldson, L., 'Social Class and the polytechnics', *Higher Education
Review*, autumn 1971.
Fogelman, K., 'Leaving the sixth form', *National Further Education
Review*, 1972.
Hoult, David A., 'The Open University: Its structure and operation',
unpublished thesis for Diploma in Education, University of Hull,
1971.
Lewis, Brian N., 'Course production at the Open University',
British Journal of Educational Technology (a series of articles: the
first appeared in vol. 2, no. 1, 1971; the fifth in the series in vol. 3,
no. 3, 1972).
Pratt, John, 'Standards in higher education', *Higher Education Review*,
autumn 1971.
Robbins, Lord, 'Reflections on eight years of expansion in higher
education,' *Higher Education*, vol. 1, no. 2, 1972.
Rogers, Jennifer, *Adults Learning* (Penguin Education) 1971.
Scupham, John, *The Open University*, London: International Broadcast
Institute (Monograph no. 1), 1972.
Trow, Martin, 'The Open University', *New Society*, 4 May 1972.
Wagner, Leslie, 'The Economics of the Open University', *Higher
Education*, May 1972.

Open University publications

Early Development of the Open University. Report of the Vice-Chancellor,
   January 1969–December 1970, The Open University, 1972.
The First Teaching Year of the Open University, Report of the
   Vice-Chancellor, 1971, The Open University, 1973.
Guide for Applicants, annually.
B.A. Degree Handbook, annually.
Postgraduate Prospectus.
Post-Experience Courses Prospectus.

Open University teaching materials

The basic correspondence units of all OU courses are on general sale
   in course book form.
Copies of all Open University/BBC television and radio programmes
   are similarly on sale (Director of Marketing, Open University,
   Walton Hall, Bletchley, Milton Keynes MK7 6AA).

Newspaper publications

Current developments may be followed in:
The Times Higher Education Supplement
Sesame (the newspaper of the Open University).

Index

Academic staff: B B C, relationship with, 116, 136–7; functions of, 115, 121, 138; part-time teachers and, 137–8; publication and, 116; publishing operation and, 137, 165–6; standards of, xii–xiii; students and, 99, 109, 120–1, 137, 138–9; *see also* Course teams

Act of Parliament: Education Act (1944), 36

Advisory Centre for Education, 3

Alexander, Professor K. J., 7

Alexander, Sir William, 11

Annan, Lord, 7

Armstrong, Sir William, 5, 15

Arts Faculty, 58, 65, 74; broadcasting and, 160, 161–2; correspondence units, 161; Foundation Course of, 158–9; second-level courses of, 159–160; third-level courses of, 161

Ashby, Sir Eric, 5, 11, 143

B B C *see* British Broadcasting Corporation

Benjamin, Walter, 'The Work of Art in the Age of its Mechanical Reproduction', 39

Benton, Senator William, 3

Bevan, Aneurin, 6

Boyle, Sir Edward, 14, 15–16

Briault, Dr E. W., 7, 11

Briggs, Professor Asa, 11, 13

British Broadcasting Corporation, 4–5, 9, 16, 35, 78, 124; College of the Air, plans for, 3, 6; Further Education Advisory Committee of, 10; O U academics and, 116, 136–7; Planning Committee, discussion with, 12–13; recruiting policy for O U broadcasts, xvi, 181

Broadcasting: arrangements with O U, future of, xix; arts Faculty and, 160; costs, xix, 23, 146, 170–2; mathematics Faculty and, 146–7, 173; other teaching methods and, vii, 123–124, 182–3; Pilkington Committee on, 5; programme preparation, 127–8; role of, 100–1, 123–4, 172–4, 182; science Faculty and, 172, 176; students, use made by, 63–4, 175; technology Faculty and, 172; time, xix, 12–13, 95, 174

Catlin, Sir George, 3

Chambers, Sir Paul, 14

Chicago College of the Air, 4

Christodoulou, Anastasios, 14, 15

Clark, Douglas, 167–8

C M A S (computer-marked assignments), 80, 81, 91, 92–3, 104

188 *Index*

College of the Air, idea of, 3, 6
Computer, 73, 127, 132, 138,
    180–1; value to ou, 181–2
Correspondence courses, vii, 123;
    post-experience courses,
    development of, 52–3; second-
    level, 86, 88, 98, 151, 156, 159;
    student reaction to, 72–3;
    texts of, 31; tutors, 127; units,
    108, 122–3, 126–7, 161; *see
    also* Course teams; Foundation
    Courses
Counsellors, 64, 67, 71–2, 79,
    95–6, 111; function of, 117
Course production, 30, 42, 125,
    128–31, 134, 158
Course Readers, 122, 131, 137,
    165
Course teams, 121–3, 167, 180–1;
    chairman of, 121–2, 133, 136,
    139; mathematics Faculty,
    145–6; outside academics,
    relationship with, 122, 160;
    social science Faculty, 135; *see
    also* Academic staff;
    Correspondence courses
Crosland, Anthony, 9
Crossman, Richard, 13
Crowther, Lord, 14

Department of Education and
    Science (des), 5, 6, 9, 15, 16,
    17, 32
Donaldson, L., 'Social Class and
    the polytechnics', *Higher
    Education Review*, 61

Education, Ministry of, 3, 5
Education Faculty, 65; Local
    Education Authorities and,
    155; Milton Keynes College of
    Education and, 157; problems
    of, 153–4; second-level courses,
    156–7

Educational technologists, 115,
    180–1
Educational Testing Service, 75
Encyclopedia Britannica, 3–4
English, Cyril, 6
Examinations, 98, 101, 111;
    structure of, 106; student
    response to, 86; time of, 95

Ferguson, Professor, 159
Foundation Courses, 75, 175;
    arts Faculty, 85, 110, 158–61;
    mathematics Faculty, 30, 145–
    148; multi-media, use in,
    126–8; preferences in, 49;
    production of, 125–6, 128–31,
    175; provisions of, 88, 118;
    science Faculty, 90, 104, 140;
    social science Faculty, 90, 97,
    110, 125, 135; technology
    Faculty, 48, 65, 149–51;
    work-load of, 64; *see also*
    Correspondence courses;
    Course teams
French, Harry, 6
Fulton, Lord, 5, 9, 11

Gaitskell, Hugh, 4
Goodman, Lord, 5, 11, 12
Greene, Sir Hugh, 13
Groombridge, Brian, 11

Heath, Edward, 16
Himmelweit, Professor Hilde T., 11
Hoggart, Richard, *The Uses of
    Literacy*, 34
Holroyde, D. J. G., 7
Hornby, Richard, 16
Hughes, I., 11

Imperial War Museum, 162
Independent Television
    Authority (ita), 9; Adult
    Education Committee of, 10

Institute of Educational
  Technology, 70–1, 76, 133

James Report on Teacher
  Education and Training
  (1972), 153
Jenkins, Roy, 15
Jones, Dr Brynmor, 7, 11

Labour Party, 35; Manifesto of
  (1964), 4; research department,
  3
Laslett, Peter, 7
Lee, Jennie, 4–7, 9–15, 37
Lewis, Brian N., 'Course
  production at the Open
  University', *British Journal of
  Educational Technology*, 132
Llewellyn, Dr F. J., 11
Llewellyn-Jones, Professor F., 7
Local Education Authorities,
  relation with OU, 68, 110–11, 155

McCarthy, M. C., 143
Mackenzie, N. I., 7, 9, 11, 13
Maclean, Roderick, 12, 13
Macleod, Iain, 16
Marketing Division of OU, 168
Mathematics Faculty, 74;
  broadcasting, 146–7, 173;
  Foundation Course, 145–8;
  higher level courses, 96;
  students, problem of
  qualifications of, 145;
  withdrawal rate, 57–8; work-
  load, 57
Media Production Department
  of OU, 129, 167

National Extension College, 3,
  78, 95, 102
National Labour College, 6
National University, idea of, 27,
  33

Open University (OU):
  admissions policy, 47–9; adult
  education and tradition of,
  34–5; advisory committee on,
  6–7; assessment system of, 73–
  75; characteristics of, vii–ix;
  social class elements of, xi,
  36–7, 40, 51, 54, 59–63, 106–
  107; costs of, ix–x, 21–4,
  30–1, 131–2, 146, 170–2;
  inter-disciplinary approach of,
  99–100, 151, 158–9; Local
  Education Authorities,
  relation with, 68, 110–11, 155;
  multi-media, use of, 180–3;
  publicity, 50–2; school leavers,
  question of admitting full-time
  to, xx, 25–7, 37, 75, 144;
  standards of, xiii, 96, 142;
  teaching methods of, vii, 31,
  122–3; traditional universities,
  relationship with, 29–30, 68;
  Treasury, difficulties with, 3,
  5, 15

Perry, Dr Walter, 14, 15, 17
Peterson, A. D., 7
Pickard, Dr O. G., 7
Pile, Sir William, 15
Pilkington Committee on
  broadcasting, 5
Planning Committee of OU, 7;
  BBC, discussion with, 12–13;
  constitution of, xv–xvi, 11–
  12; predictions of, 15, 153–4;
  Report to the Secretary of
  State for Education and
  Science (1969), xi–xii, 13–14
Playfair, Lyon, 142
Plowden, Lady, 15
Postgate, Richmond, 6
Pratt, John, 'Standards in higher
  education', *Higher Education
  Review*, 29

Project Control of ou, 168
Publishing Division of ou, 167

Readers and Set Books, 167
Richmond, Dr A. J., 12
Ritchie-Calder, Professor Lord, 12
Robbins, Lord, 5; Committee of, 23, 29; Report of, 34, 61

Saturday schools, 67, 69
Science Faculty, 39, 74; aims of, 144; broadcasting, 172, 176; Foundation Course, 90, 104, 140; teaching methods, 141–2; withdrawal rate, 57; work-load, 57, 64–5
Scupham, John, 6, 7, 11, 12
Shaw, Professor Roy, 5, 12
Short, Edward, 13, 14, 16, 37
Social science Faculty, 39, 58, 74; broadcasting, 136–7; Foundation Course, 65, 90, 97, 110, 125, 135; Reader, production of, 137; summer schools, 118, 138
Soviet Union, 3
Students: age of, 55; broadcasting, use made by, 63–4; 175; social class of, xi, 36–7, 40, 51, 54, 59–63, 106–107; cost per, 21–5; educational qualifications of, 47–8, 56–8; family, effect upon, 87–8, 91, 92–3, 95–6, 112; geographical pattern of, 48; growth rate of, 69; isolation of, 79, 97, 110–12, 173; learning difficulties of, 77–9, 172–3; motives of, 81, 89, 94, 95, 97–8, 102, 107; occupation of, 56, 147, 153; withdrawal rate of, xvii, 57, 59; work-load of, 30, 57, 64–5, 78, 97, 102–3

Study centres, 69, 71, 88, 97, 99, 105; role of, 79, 93, 106–7, 118, 171; students, use made by, 63–4, 103, 111
Summer schools, 66, 79–80, 105, 108–9, 118, 148, *et passim*
Supplementary Material booklets, 166

Technology faculty, 38; broadcasting, 172; Foundation Course, 149–52
Thatcher, Margaret, 15, 16, 17
tmas (tutor-marked assignments), 81, 91, 92–3, 102, 104
Toomey, Ralph, 6
Tutors, xix, 68, 71–2, 105, 136; staff tutors, relationship with, 117, 127, 138, *et passim*

United States, 35–6, 37, 75, 178–180
University of the Air, 87, 178; advisory committee on, 6–7; idea of, 3; report by advisory committee, 7–9; White Paper on, 6; Wilson's pre-election speech on, 4
University Grants Committee, 9

Venables, Sir Peter, 10–15, 17

Wagner, Leslie, 'The Economics of the Open University', *Higher Education*, 21, 30
Walton Hall, 16, 69, 99, 109, 111, 115, 137
wea *see* Workers' Educational Association
Weekend schools, 41, 103
White Paper on *A University of the Air* (1966), 182
Williams, Raymond, *Culture and Society*, 34

Williams, Shirley, 32
Wilson, Harold, 3–4, 15, 16, 37
Wiltshire, Professor Harold, 7,
  11, 12

Workers' Educational
  Association, 4, 9, 51, 68, 85

Young, Dr Michael, 3